365 TiNY
Cross Stitch
Designs

by Kooler Design Studio

Bobbie Matela, Managing Editor
Carol Wilson Mansfield, Art Director
Carly Poggemeyer, Editorial Director
Pam Nichols, Editor
Lisa DeLasaux, Jane Cannon Meyers,
    Glenda Tucker, and Christina Wilson,
    Editorial Assistants
Mary Hernandez, Book Design

Cross stitch charts by:
Rick Causee, Mary Hernandez,
Kyle Nichols, Pam Nichols,
Carly Poggemeyer, and
Brent Rathburn.

Photographed models were stitched by:
Jill Brooks, Linda Causee,
Barbara Chancy, Jessica Chism,
Carrie Christiano, Betty Curran,
Maryann Donovan, Millie Fortner,
Ellen Harnden, Sandi Kardack,
Janet Kazmer, Sue McVae,
Maxine Meadows, Pam Nichols,
Jan Orantes, Carly Poggemeyer,
Sandy Scoville, Lee Ann Tibbals,
Christina Wilson, and Nancy Withrow.

For a full-color catalog including books of cross stitch designs, write to:

American School of Needlework®
Consumer Division
1455 Linda Vista Drive
San Marcos, CA 92069

or visit us at http://www.asnpub.com

©2000 by Kooler Design Studio, Inc.
Published by American School of Needlework®, Inc.
ASN Publishing, 1455 Linda Vista Drive, San Marcos, CA 92069

ISBN: 0-88195-943-X   Library of Congress Control Number: 2003100303   All rights reserved.   7 8 9

Introduction

Owning this book is a cross stitcher's dream come true!

No matter what the occasion, season or holiday, you'll always have quick-to-stitch small designs to stitch up in a hurry!

365 Tiny Cross Stitch Designs is a fun-to-peruse and easy-to-use volume featuring creations by the fabulous Kooler Design Studio needlework artists. Each month has its own chapter of designs—with a design for each day of the year. We've even included a bonus leap year design in February, making our audited total a whopping 366 designs.

Notice that our months have certain themes in common. In each month you'll find a teapot, a zodiac sign, a wreath, a flower of the month, a fairy of the month, a countrified mini sampler and a little patchwork quilt design. These are all shown in framed groupings on the back cover and on pages 6 to 10.

Tradition abounds with these beautiful flowers. A chart for a Flower of the Month can be found on the 2nd of each month.

3

Table of Contents

January

Happy New Year! Celebrate your resolutions with a quick-to-stitch project this January.

Photo Gallery
pages 12-13

Charts
pages 14-22

February

Show the love in your heart by stitching a Valentines's Day gift for that special someone.

Photo Gallery
pages 24-25

Charts
pages 26-34

March

It may still be a little chilly, but you can welcome the coming spring with a new design to stitch.

Photo Gallery
pages 36-37

Charts
pages 38-46

April

Spring showers will soon give us glorious gardens. And don't forget Easter.

Photo Gallery
pages 48-49

Charts
pages 50-58

May

Mother's Day is upon us before we know it, but these little designs are wonderful gifts for the moms in our lives.

Photo Gallery
pages 60-61

Charts
pages 62-70

June

So many events this month; graduations, Father's Day and weddings! There is plenty of time to stitch a tiny design.

Photo Gallery
pages 72-73

Charts
pages 74-82

July

Picnics, fireworks, and the Fourth of July are wonderful ways to celebrate this month.

August

Summer is hot and you can relax with a cool glass of lemonade in the shade while stitching your favorite designs.

September

Now it's back to school time and autumn is on the way. Stitch a gift for your child's favorite teacher.

October

The ghosts and goblins are out and about the end of this month. But don't forget autumn and all its luscious colors.

November

The year is almost over, and there's much for which to be thankful. Show your gratitude to a favorite person with a quick handcrafted gift.

December

During the hustle and bustle of the holiday season, be sure to take time to cross stitch a design for yourself!

Quilt Block of the Month

These designs appeal to the quilt lovers in all of us. A chart for a Quilt Block of the Month can be found on the 12th of each month.

Zodiac Sign of the Month

What's your sign? No matter which
it is, the design is sure to please you.
A chart for a Zodiac Sign of the Month
can be found on the 10th of each month.

Mini Sampler of the Month

Celebrate your favorite month with these country samplers. A chart for a Mini Sampler of the Month can be found on the 8th of each month.

Wreath of the Month

Add a wonderful holiday touch to your home with your favorite wreath. A chart for a Wreath of the Month can be found on the 6th of each month.

Teapot of the Month

A new twist on the ritual of tea drinking is cleverly demonstrated in these teapots. A chart for a Teapot of the Month can be found on the 16th of each month.

Birthstone Fairy of the Month

Each fairy delights in presenting you with
your favorite birthstone. A chart for a
Birthstone Fairy of the Month can be found
on the 28th of each month.

January

January 27

January 3

January 16

January 28

GARNET

January 6

January 5

January 9

January 4

January 19

January 21

January 31

DOG MOM

January 30

January 7

friends

January 18

WELCOME

January 17

January

January 10

January 8

January 2

January 1

January 25

January 23

January 13

January 14

January 20

January 26

January 15

January 11

January 24

January 29

January 22

January 12

January 1

Design size: 32 wide x 37 high

Anchor	DMC	Backstitch:
92	553	**92** (2 strands)—"New," streamers
386	3823	**365/435**—champagne
301	744	**131** (2 strands)—"Happy,"
363	436	streamers, date
131	798	110 (2 strands)—"Year,"
110	208	streamers
234	762	400/317—glasses

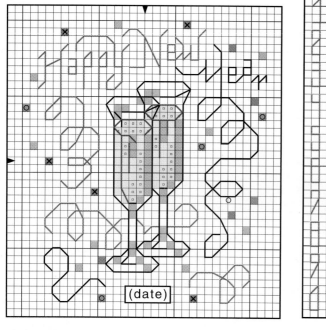

(date)

January 2

Design size: 28 wide x 30 high

Anchor	DMC	Anchor	DMC
24	963	843	3012
27	899	**French Knot:** 29	
29	309	**Backstitch:**	
259	772	29—flower, "Carnation"	
265	3347	44/815—border, "JANUARY"	
257	905	246/986—leaves	
842	3013	845/730—stem	

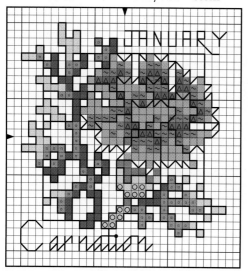

January 3

Design size: 21 wide x 25 high

Anchor	DMC	Backstitch:
2	blanc	**76/961**—heart
73	963	302/743(2 strands)—
386	3823	halo
293	727	306/783—wings
128	800	**349/301**—hair
French Knots:		400/317—remaining
403/310		outlines

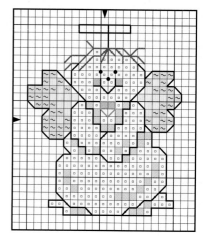

January 4

Design size: 17 wide x 32 high

Anchor	DMC	Backstitch:
2	blanc	334—collar
334	606	**211/562**—pine needles
128	800	369/435—branch
367	738	400/317—bird, bear
403	310	(except nose)
French Knot: 403		403—nose

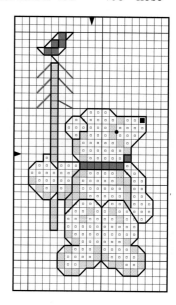

January 5

Design size: 21 wide x 22 high

Anchor	DMC	French Knot: 403/310
2	blanc	**Backstitch:**
334	606	**334**—scarf fringe
46	666	211/562—branch
9159	828	400—remaining
1038/1039	519/518	outlines
400	317	

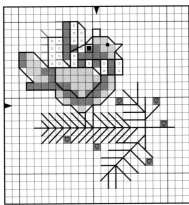

January 6

Design size: 29 wide x 29 high

Anchor	DMC	Backstitch:
2	blanc	333/608—ribbon,
332	946	orange ornaments &
85	3609	confetti
87	3607	268/469—wreath
78	3685	188—turquoise
328	3341	ornaments & confetti
265	3347	101/550—balloon,
1092	995	purple ornaments &
186	959	confetti
188	3812	403—lettering, string,
403	310	checks

January 7

Design size: 22 wide x 26 high

Anchor	DMC	French Knot: 403
2	blanc	**Backstitch:**
24	963	349/301—car (except
334	606	wheels)
301	744	400/317—mouse
313	742	(except nose),
129	809	clothes, wheels
2/234	blanc/762	403—nose
399	318	
403	310	

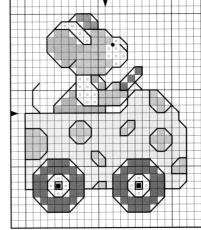

January 8

Design size: 25 wide x 38 high

Anchor	DMC	Backstitch:
2	blanc	121—snowflakes, bottom
108	210	zigzag, "SNOW," "SN"
159	3325	121 (2 strands)—bottom line
121	809	1030/3746—ice outlines,
236	3799	top zigzag, "ICE," "ICE,"
French Knots: 236		bottom motif
		1030 (2 strands)—line under
		bottom motif
		236—"JAN," trees

January 9

Design size: 27 wide x 29 high

	Anchor	DMC		Anchor	DMC
□	2	blanc	■	236	3799
■	334	606			
□	300	745			
■	313	742			
~	240	966			
■	242	989			
■	928	3811			
⊙	129	809			
■	146	798			
■	398	415			

French Knots: 403/310
Straight Stitch:
146—scarf fringe
Backstitch:
334—hat stripes
146—scarf
370/434—fishing pole
400/317—remaining
　outlines

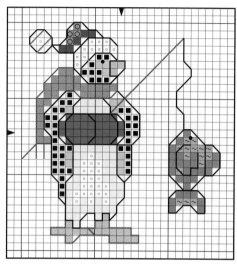

January 10

Design size: 33 wide x 29 high

	Anchor	DMC		Anchor	DMC
□	2	blanc	■	1048	3776
■	1092	995	■	231	453
⊙	186	959	■	233	452
■	188	3812	■	403	310
□	311	3827		**Backstitch:** 403	
~	1002	977			

January 11

Design size: 25 wide x 34 high

	Anchor	DMC
□	2	blanc
~	85	3609
■	108	210
□	128	800
■	130	809
■	1092	995
△	185/186	964/959
□	881	945
■	378	841

French Knots:
130—snowflakes
403/310—eye, nose
Backstitch:
130—snowflakes
1049/3826—bear
400/317—remaining
　outlines

January 12

Design size: 30 wide x 30 high

	Anchor	DMC
□	2	blanc
■	98	553
~	129	809
■	131	798

Backstitch: 400/317

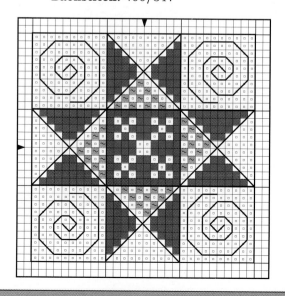

January 13

Design size: 28 wide x 30 high

Anchor	DMC
2	blanc
95	554
1020	3713
1092	995
130	809
136	799
108	210

French Knots: 403/310
Backstitch:
136—ark stripes, string
400/317—remaining outlines

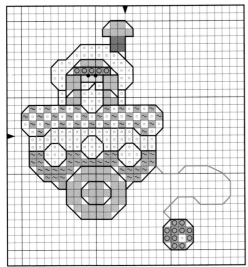

January 15

Design size: 28 wide x 28 high

Anchor	DMC	Anchor	DMC
2	blanc	349	301
300	745	351	400
302	743		
314	741		
925	971		
875	3813		
876	3816		
879	500		
347	402		

Backstitch:
2—orange section lines (except center)
925—orange center & outlines
879—leaves, green on orange
351—branches, stems

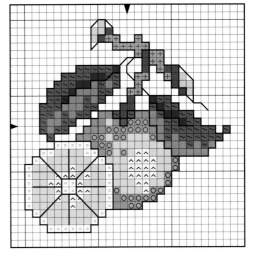

January 14

Design size: 31 wide x 24 high

Anchor	DMC	Anchor	DMC
2	blanc	96	3609
334	606	956	613
295	726	1048	3776
329	3340	234	762
208	563	235	414
128	800	403	310
130	809		

Backstitch: 403

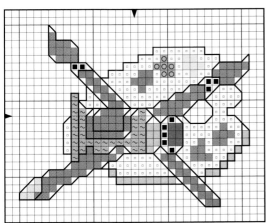

January 16

Design size: 35 wide x 30 high

Anchor	DMC	Anchor	DMC
2	blanc	129	809
46	666	142	798
314	741	403	310
332	946		
292	3078		
302	743		
261	989		
246	986		
128	800		

Backstitch:
47/321—bird (except beak)
246—leaves
139/797—teapot, snow
403—beak

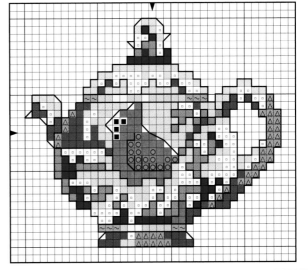

January 17

Design size: 69 wide x 20 high

Anchor	DMC
276	739
73	963
895	223
367	738

Backstitch:
1027/3722—heart, lettering
369/435—banner

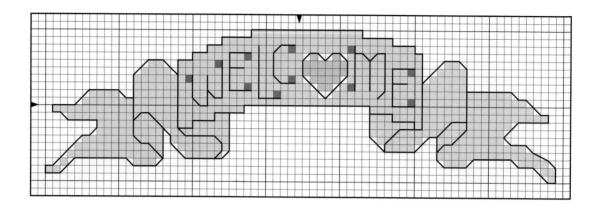

January 18

Design size: 51 wide x 28 high

Anchor	DMC
2	blanc
24	963
95	554
96	3609
311	3827
240	966
227	701
276	739
367	738

Anchor	DMC
370	434
403	310

French Knots:
162/517—lettering
403—eye

Backstitch:
162—lettering
370—mouse, pen clip & nib
400/317—clothes, remaining pen

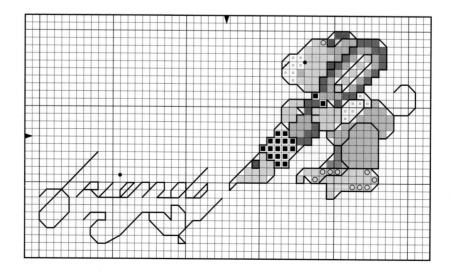

January 19

Design size: 19 wide x 23 high

Anchor	DMC	French Knot: 403/310
2	blanc	**Backstitch:**
334	606	**47**—scarf fringe
47	321	210/562—lines on cup,
206	564	branch
361	738	400/317—remaining
1080	842	outlines
1082	841	

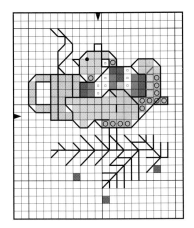

January 20

Design size: 27 wide x 18 high

Anchor	DMC
334	606
1012	754
301	744
129	809
1047	402
1048	3776

French Knots:
146/798—baby
1049/3826—bear

Backstitch:
1024/3328—mouth
1013/3778—skin, hair, nose
1049—bear
400/317—clothes, shoe

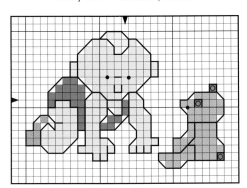

January 21

Design size: 33 wide x 10 high

Anchor	DMC
2	blanc
24	963
2/234	blanc/762
399	318
235	414

French Knot: 403
Backstitch:
38/961—yarn
400/317—cat (except nose)
403/310—nose

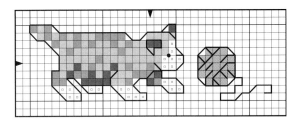

January 22

Design size: 18 wide x 34 high

Anchor	DMC
2	blanc
73	963
75	962
77	3687
386	3823
305	743
313	742
209	913
128	800
130	809
403	310

Backstitch:
349/301—flame
400/317—remaining outlines

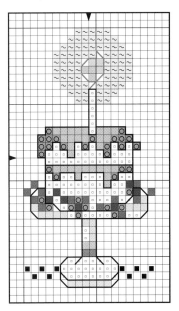

January 23

Design size: 21 wide x 30 high

	Anchor	DMC
▫	2	blanc
▨	73	963
☐	301	744
☐	302	743
☐	1031	3753
▨	1033	932
■	403	310

Backstitch:
76/961—star nose
1001/976—star (except eyes & mouth)
145/809—moon (except eye)
403—eyes, star mouth

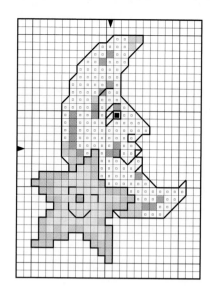

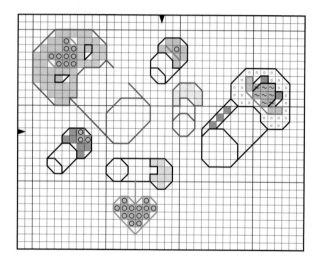

January 24

Design size: 35 wide x 27 high

	Anchor	DMC
▫	2	blanc
◉	74	3354
▨	85	3609
▨	8	3824
☐	293	727
▨	206	564
▨	1092	995
☐	120	3747
∼	103	211

Backstitch:
76/961—hearts, heart string
209/913—leaves
109/209—flower
349/301—diaper pins
400/317—remaining diaper pins

January 25

Design size: 36 wide x 29 high

	Anchor	DMC
▫	2	blanc
▨	158	747
☐	933	543
▨	1008	3773
▲	1007	3772
▨	234	762
▨	399	318
■	403	310

Eyelets:
977/3755—stars

Backstitch:
977—snow, lettering
876/3816—trees
400/317—cabin

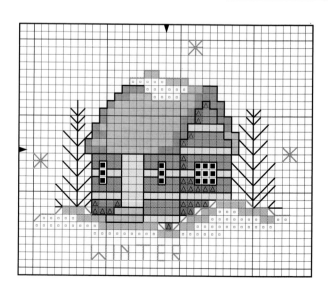

January 26

Design size: 21 wide x 32 high

	Anchor	DMC
☐	300	745
☐	311	3827
☐	214	368
☐	108	210

French Knots: 400/317
Backstitch:
217/561—leaves, stems
400—remaining outlines

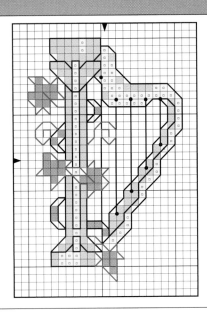

January 27

Design size: 32 wide x 34 high

	Anchor	DMC
☐	2	blanc
☐	73	963
~	386	3823
◎	293	727
☐	297	973
☐	313	742
☐	1003	922
☐	108	210

French Knots: 403/310
Backstitch:
1049/3826—crown, tiger (except muzzle)
400/317—robe
403/310—muzzle

January 28

Design size: 23 wide x 41 high

	Anchor	DMC		Anchor	DMC
☐	2	blanc	◎	1048	3776
☐	24	963	☐	1004	920
♡	50	605	☐	259	772
☐	46	666	~	265	3347
☐	1006	304	☐	262	3363
☐	20	815			
☐	1012	754			
☐	868	353			
☐	332	946			
☐	300	745			
+	311	3827			
☐	1002	977			

Backstitch:
26/894—wings
1006—"GARNET"
20—gem, red part of dress
1004—skin, hair
262—remaining dress
403/310—eyes

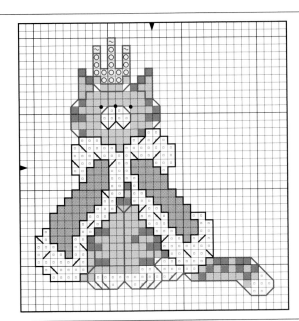

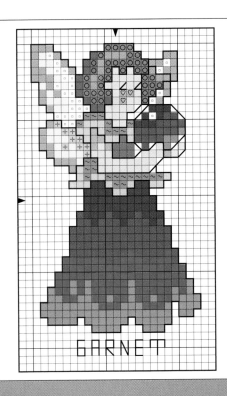

January 29

Design size: 43 wide x 18 high

	Anchor	DMC
▫	2	blanc
□	276	739
▨	1032	3752
▨	366	951
▨	368	437
▨	370	434
▨	399	318
■	403	310

Backstitch:
370—cat (except eye), tree
235/414—snow
403—cat eye, bird

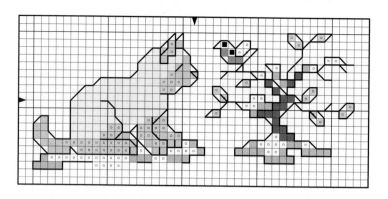

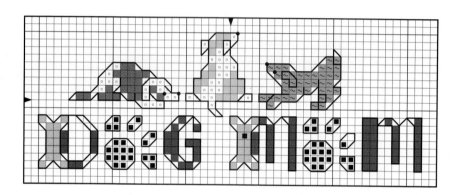

January 30

Design size: 52 wide x 18 high

	Anchor	DMC
▫	2	blanc
▨	347	402
▨	362	437
▨	370	434
~	891	676
▨	899	3782
■	403	310

French Knots: 403
Backstitch:
371/434—letters, bones
400/317—dogs
403—pawprints

January 31

Design size: 29 wide x 36 high

	Anchor	DMC
▫	2	blanc
▨	334	606
■	1005	816
⊞	300	745
□	305	743
□	311	3827
~	314	741
□	128	775
△	129	800
▨	130	809
□	881	945
◎	368	437
⊠	1047	402
▨	370	434
▨	398	415
▨	235	414
■	403	310

French Knot: 403
Backstitch:
1049/3826—bear (except nose),
   snowshoes (except straps)
400/317—clothes, hat, mittens, boots
403—lantern, snowshoe straps, nose

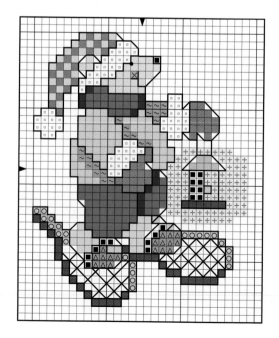

February

February 23

February 7

February 25

February 16

February 22

February 20

February 3

February 5

February 19

February 27

February 15

February 26

February 21

cats are my favorite people

February 2

24

February

February 28 — AMETHYST

February 10 — AQUARIUS

February 6 — BE MINE

February 8 — FEB / LOVE·LOVE·LOVE

February 1

February 24

February 14

February 13

February 17

February 4

February 18

February 9

February 11 — BASKETBALL

February 29 — 29

February 12

February 1

Design size: 24 wide x 18 high

Anchor	DMC	Backstitch:
▫ 2	blanc	**146/798**—thread
■ 334	606	306/783—needle
▫ 128	800	400/317—heart
■ 403	310	

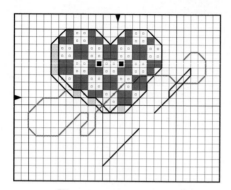

February 2

Design size: 28 wide x 29 high

Anchor	DMC
▫ 302	743
▫ 259	772
△ 265	3347
■ 257	905
▫ 1031	3753
~ 1092	995
▫ 2/342	blanc/211
◎ 95/108	554/210
■ 109	209

French Knot: 109
Backstitch:
246/986—leaves, stems
109—"Violet"
110/208—violets
111/553—"FEBRUARY"
236/3799—border

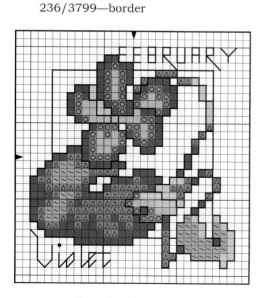

February 3

Design size: 35 wide x 22 high

Anchor	DMC		Anchor	DMC
▫ 2	blanc		~ 387	712
▫ 95	554		▫ 336	758
▫ 361	738		■ 338	922
◎ 362	437			
▫ 1043	369			
▫ 206	564			

French Knots: 403/310
Backstitch: 400/317

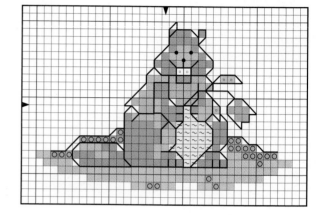

February 4

Design size: 30 wide x 27 high

Anchor	DMC
▫ 2	blanc
▫ 25	3326
■ 26/38	894/961
▫ 300	745
▫ 311	3827
■ 242	989
▫ 975	3753
◎ 343	3752

French Knots: 403/310
Backstitch: 400/317

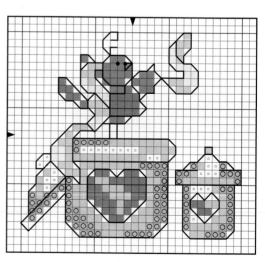

February 5

Design size: 29 wide x 25 high

	Anchor	DMC		Anchor	DMC
⊙	73	963	☐	881	945
☐	103	211	☐	1047	402
	96	3609			
☐	386	3823			
⊡	301	744			
	1092	995			
△	185	964			
☐	128	800			
	129	809			

French Knots: 403/310
Backstitch:
76/961—heart
1049/3826—bears
400/317—remaining
    outlines

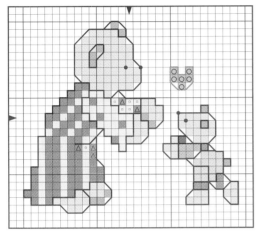

February 6

Design size: 29 wide x 31 high

	Anchor	DMC
▫	2	blanc
☐	27	899
	46	666
	1005	816
	259	772
	265	3347
△	268	469

Backstitch:
1005—hearts, lettering
268—leaves, tendrils

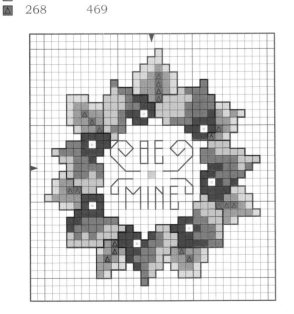

February 7

Design size: 18 wide x 19 high

	Anchor	DMC
▫	2	blanc
☐	1012	754
☐	301	744
☐	305	743
☐	128	800
	130	809
☐	342	211

French Knots: 349/301
Backstitch:
1024/3328—mouth
1013/3778—skin, nose
109/209—dress stripes
349—hair
400/317—remaining
    outlines

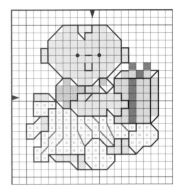

February 8

Design size: 25 wide x 38 high

	Anchor	DMC
∼	275	746
⊡	1022	760
	39	309
	43	814
■	400	317

French Knots: 39

Backstitch:
39—"FEB," stamps,
    valentine writing
    lines, heart hangers
39 (2 strands)—motif
    division lines
43—arrows
400—remaining
    outlines

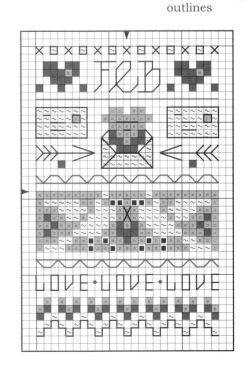

February 9

Design size: 21 wide x 19 high

	Anchor	DMC
▫	2	blanc
▨	74	3354
☐	301	744
▨	302	743

Backstitch:
370/434—ribbon
400/317—hearts

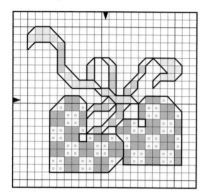

February 10

Design size: 32 wide x 30 high

	Anchor	DMC
▫	2	blanc
▨	1002	977
▨	1048	3776
☐	1092	995
☐	185	964
~	187	958
△	188	3812
■	403	310

Backstitch:
189/943—water
403—pitcher, lettering

February 11

Design size: 22 wide x 24 high

	Anchor	DMC
▨	1047	402
▨	1048	3776
▨	234	762
■	403	310

Backstitch:
334/606—"BALL"
146/798—"BASKET"
1049/3826—ball outline, netting
403—remaining ball, basket rim

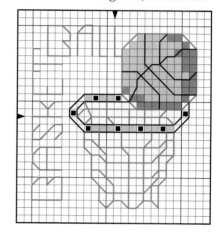

February 12

Design size: 30 wide x 30 high

	Anchor	DMC
▫	2	blanc
☐	48	3689
◉	52	957
▨	46	666
▨	43	814
☐	259	772
△	260	3364
▨	186	959
☐	159	3325
~	342	211

Backstitch: 400/317

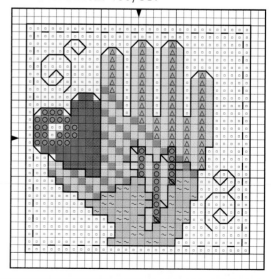

February 13

Design size: 26 wide x 22 high

Anchor	DMC	French Knot: 403/310
2	blanc	**Backstitch:**
23	3713	162—umbrella (except
46	666	tip & cheese)
300	745	1049/3826—cheese,
1002	977	umbrella tip, mouse
311	3827	(except face)
881	945	403—face, shirt
160	827	
162	517	

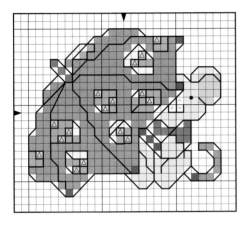

February 14

Design size: 29 wide x 31 high

Anchor	DMC	
24	963	1046/435—yellow
301	744	hearts & beads
206	564	205/912—green
342	211	hearts & beads
French Knots: 400/317		110/208—purple
Lazy Daisy: 400 (2 strands)		heart & beads,
Backstitch:		thread
57/602—pink hearts		400—lettering
& beads		400 (2 strands)—
		needle point

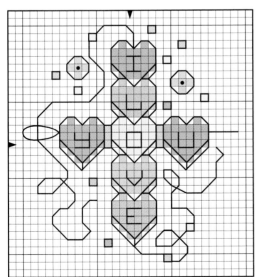

February 15

Design size: 28 wide x 25 high

Anchor	DMC
2	blanc
24	963
388	3033
370	434
234	762
403	310

Backstitch:
400/317—dog, (except eyes & nose), bug
403—eyes, nose

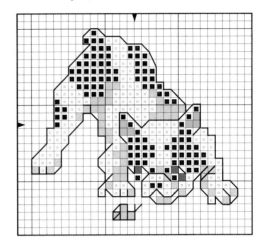

February 16

Design size: 35 wide x 29high

Anchor	DMC	Anchor	DMC
2	blanc	185	964
23	3713	128	800
27	899	**Backstitch:**	
29	309	29—lid, pink flowers	
314	741	332/946—heart ribbon	
301	744	845—leaves	
302	743	188/3812—turquoise	
843	3012	flowers	
845	730	136/799—remaining teapot	

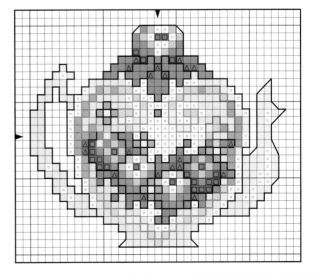

February 17

Design size: 22 wide x 30 high

Anchor	DMC
2	blanc
387	712
334	606
73	963
311	3827
1031	3753
881	945
403	310

French Knots: 403
Backstitch:
210/562—stems
1049/3826—bear (except nose), purse clasp
400/317—dress, socks, remaining purse
403—nose, shoes

February 18

Design size: 8 wide x 50 high

Anchor	DMC
2	blanc
334	606
96	3609
305	743
314	741
185	964
128	800
403	310

Backstitch:
349/301—flame
400/317—remaining outlines

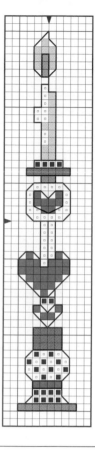

February 19

Design size: 52 wide x 30 high

Anchor	DMC		Anchor	DMC
2	blanc		881	945
73	963		1047	402
75	962		234	762
334	606		403	310
305	743			
387	712			

French Knot: 403

Backstitch:
76/961—lt pink hearts
77/3687—med pink hearts
1005/816—red hearts
1049/3826—bear (except nose)
400/317—wagon
403—nose

February 20

Design size: 41 wide x 26 high

	Anchor	DMC			Anchor	DMC
▫	2	blanc		▫	367	437
■	334	606		▫	361	738
▫	295	726		◎	363	436
▫	128	800		△	369	435
▨	130	809		■	403	310
■	1074	992			**Backstitch:** 400/317

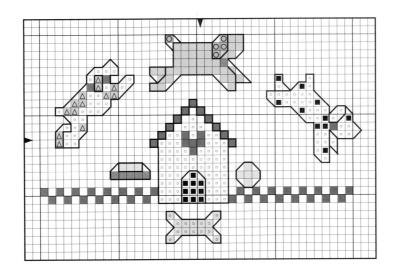

February 21

Design size: 53 wide x 13 high

	Anchor	DMC
▫	2	blanc
▨	928	3811
▫	881	945
▨	1047	402
▫	234	762
▨	235	414
■	403	310

French Knot: 1074/992
Backstitch:
1074/992—lettering
1049/3826—calico cat (except eyes)
403—eyes, gray cat

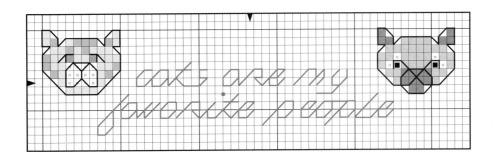

February 22

Design size: 28 wide x 29 high

	Anchor	DMC
▫	2	blanc
▨	50	605
▢	1012	754
◉	868	353
~	300	745
▢	1043	369
▨	241	966
▢	158	747
▲	167	519
▨	108	210

French Knots: 400/317
Straight Stitch (scarf fringe):—400
Backstitch: 400

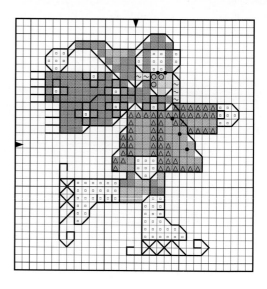

February 23

Design size: 25 wide x 34 high

	Anchor	DMC
▫	2	blanc
▨	26	894
▨	28	892
▢	128	800
▨	379	840

French Knots: 28
Backstitch:
28—ribbon
28—laces, toe lines, heart
400/317—remaining outlines

February 24

Design size: 32 wide x 26 high

	Anchor	DMC
▫	2	blanc
▨	328	3341
▢	301	744
▢	852	3047
▨	853	372
▢	1031	3753
▢	397	3024
▨	900	648
~	1040	647
▲	8581	646

French Knots: 8581
Backstitch:
333/608—doors, windows
211/562—grass
8581—remaining outlines

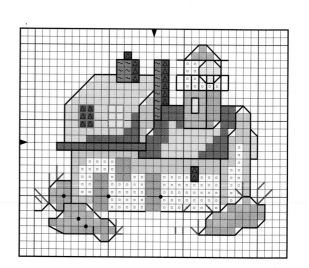

February 25

Design size: 23 wide x 34 high

	Anchor	DMC
▫	2	blanc
▨	73	963
▨	75	962
▨	1012	754
☐	301	744
▨	120	3747

French Knots: 146/798
Backstitch:
1024/3328—mouth
1013/3778—skin, nose
349/301—hair
400/317—remaining outlines

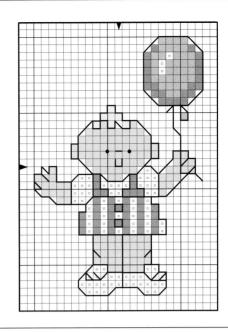

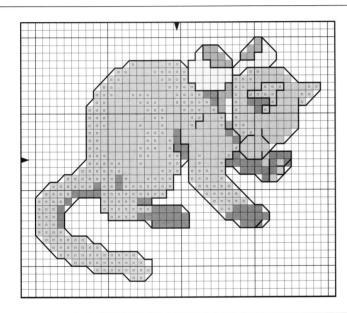

February 26

Design size: 39 wide x 32 high

	Anchor	DMC
☐	23	3713
☐	300	745
▨	890	729
▨	2/234	blanc/762
▫	398	415
▨	235	414

Backstitch:
400/317—cat (except eye), bow
403/310—eye

February 27

Design size: 29 wide x 31 high

	Anchor	DMC
▫	2	blanc
～	9	352
■	334	606
⊘	313	742
▨	241	966
▨	161	813
▨	391	3033
▫	368	437
☐	361	738
⊠	362/363	437/436
▨	400	317
■	403	310

French Knots: 403
Backstitch:
370/434—dog (except nose), hanging toy, biscuits
400—doghouse, bowl, balls, bag, pillow, toy hanger
403—nose

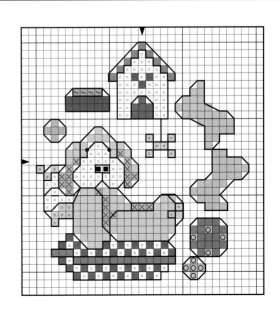

February 28

Design size: 23 wide x 42 high

	Anchor	DMC
▫	2	blanc
♡	50	605
~	103	211
▣	96	3609
⊠	99	553
♥	102	550
▨	1012	754
☐	300	745
▨	311	3827
▨	1002	997
▨	160	827
◉	161	813
▫	342	211
⊘	108/109	210/209
✚	110	208
◣	112	552

Backstitch:
1001/976—hair, skin, ribbon
102—gem
162/517—dress trim
109—wings
112—hair band, remaining dress, "AMETHYST"
403/310—eyes

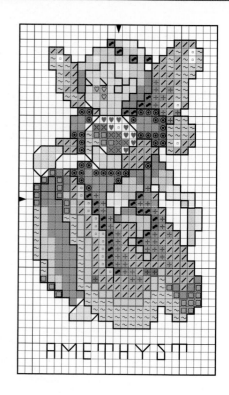

February 29

Design size: 41 wide x 34 high

	Anchor	DMC
▫	2	blanc
☐	305	743
▨	1043	369
▨	241	966
▨	234	762
■	403	310

Backstitch:
210/562—frog (except eyes, nose, mouth, chin, belly)
400/317—remaining frog (except eyes), motion lines
403—eyes, number

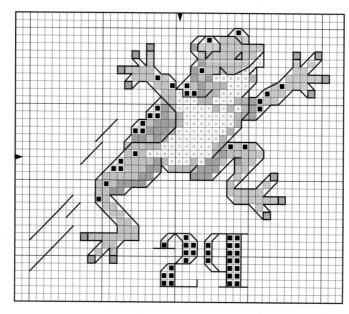

March 10

March 1

March 16

March 2

March 14

March 31

March 15

March 5

March 23

March 17

March 7

March 25

March 27

March 13

March 3

March

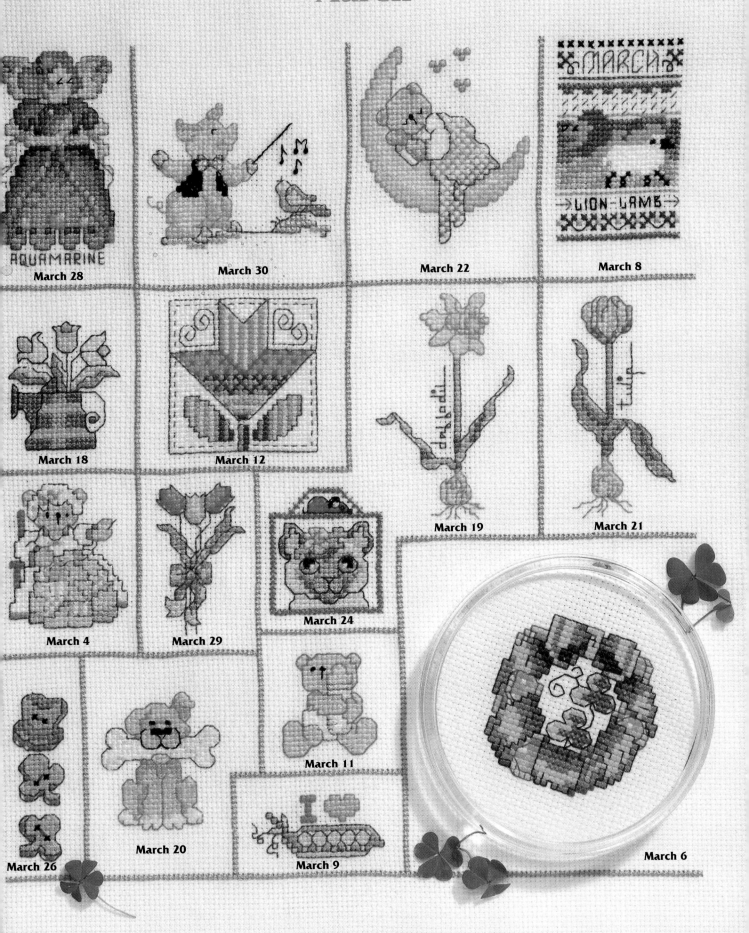

March 28

March 30

March 22

March 8

March 18

March 12

March 19

March 21

March 4

March 29

March 24

March 11

March 26

March 20

March 9

March 6

37

March 1

Design size: 31 wide x 30 high

	Anchor	DMC
□	2	blanc
☐	300	745
▣	311	3827
▨	362	437
◎	363	436
☐	128	800
▨	397	3024

French Knots: 400/317
Backstitch:
244/702—"MARCH"
400—remaining outlines

March 2

Design size: 28 wide x 30 high

	Anchor	DMC
☐	300	745
▨	302	743
▨	1003	922
▨	206	564
▨	208	563
■	211	562
■	370	434

French Knot: 1003
Backstitch:
211—leaves, stems
1003—"Daffodil"
1004/920—flower, "MARCH"
360/898—border

March 3

Design size: 24 wide x 17 high

	Anchor	DMC
□	2	blanc
▨	23	3713
▨	1047	402
▨	1048	3776
▨	234	762

Backstitch:
400/317—cat (except eyes)
403/310—eyes

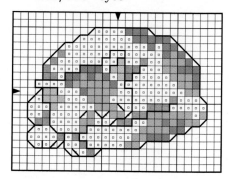

March 4

Design size: 24 wide x 28 high

	Anchor	DMC
□	2	blanc
∼	75	962
▨	85	3609
☐	1043	369
△	206	564
▨	1092	995
☐	128	800
☐	881	945
▨	349	301

French Knots: 403/310
Backstitch:
1074/992—thread
349—bear (except nose), chair
403—nose
400/317—remaining outlines

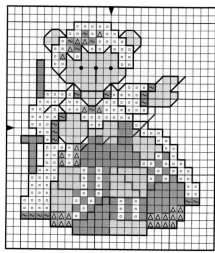

March 5

Design size: 17 wide x 19 high

	Anchor	DMC
☐	1043	369
◉	241	966
☐	9159	828
■	403	310

French Knots: 210/562
Backstitch:
210—frog (except eyes)
403—eyes

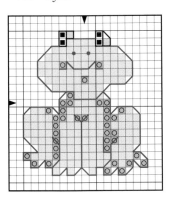

March 7

Design size: 20 wide x 20 high

	Anchor	DMC
▫	2	blanc
☐	73	963
☐	386	3823
☐	311	3827
☐	206	564
∼	342	211
▨	109	209

Backstitch:
210/562—leaves, stem
119/333—remaining outlines

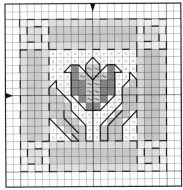

March 6

Design size: 29 wide x 28 high

	Anchor	DMC
▫	2	blanc
☐	301	744
☐	302	743
☐	314	741
☐	253	472
☐	238	703
◮	227	701
☐	246	986
∼	361	738
◉	1048	3776
▨	351	400

Backstitch:
246—ribbon, shamrocks, tendrils
351—remaining outlines

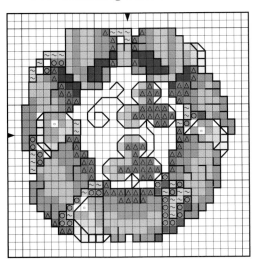

March 8

Design size: 25 wide x 38 high

	Anchor	DMC	Backstitch:
▫	2	blanc	212—clover stems
☐	206	564	**779**—rain, arrows, dash
∼	208	563	**779** (2 strands)—line
▨	212	561	under "MARCH"
▨	850/168	926/3810	368 (2 strands)—lines
☐	779	3809	above and below animals
☐	368	437	358—"MARCH"
▨	358	801	403—lion nose, remaining
■	403	310	lettering

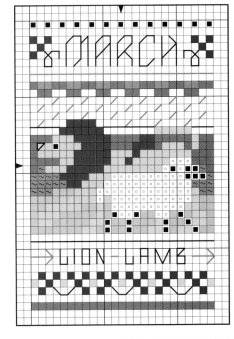

March 9

Design size: 27 wide x 12 high

Anchor	DMC
74	3354
76	961
1043	369
241	966

Backstitch:
76—heart, "I"
210/562—remaining outlines

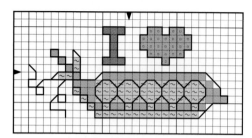

March 10

Design size: 29 wide x 33 high

Anchor	DMC
259	772
265	3347
268	469
129	809
131	798
342	211
109	209
403	310

Backstitch: 403

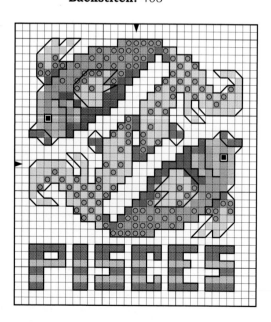

March 11

Design size: 19 wide x 20 high

Anchor	DMC
2	blanc
6	754
128	800
1092	995
881	945

French Knots: 403/310
Backstitch:
11/351—bottle nipple
1049/3826—bear (except nose)
235/414—remaining bottle, diaper
403—nose

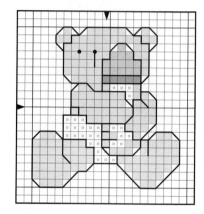

March 12

Design size: 30 wide x 30 high

Anchor	DMC
2	blanc
48	3689
52	957
46	666
259	772
265	3347
268	469

Backstitch: 400/317

March 13

Design size: 24 wide x 17 high

Anchor	DMC
2	blanc
73	963
323	3825
240	966
366	951
368	437
370	434
403	310

French Knot: 403
Backstitch:
210/562—carrot top
370—rabbit (except
    eye & muzzle),
    remaining carrot
403—eye, muzzle

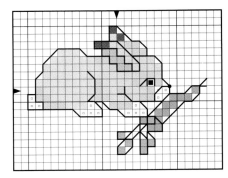

March 14

Design size: 27 wide x 34 high

Anchor	DMC
2	blanc
8	3824
11	351
302	743
2/234	blanc/762
399	318

French Knots: 401/413
Backstitch:
187/958—kite string, bows
401—mouse, kite

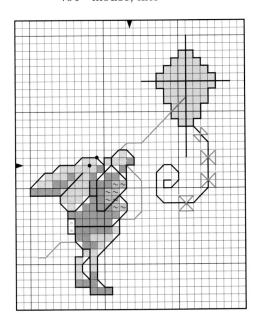

March 15

Design size: 18 wide x 19 high

Anchor	DMC
301	744
302	743
323	3825
329	3340
128	800
129	809
403	310

Backstitch:
146/798—bow
349/301—chick (except eye)
403—eye

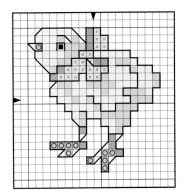

March 16

Design size: 31 wide x 27 high

Anchor	DMC
2	blanc
301	744
302	743
314	741
238	703
228	700
1047	402
1048	3776
231	453
233	452

Backstitch:
246/986—hat (except
    band), bow & neck
    band, clover, stem
1048—gold
1049/3826—cat
    (except face)
403/310—hat band,
    face, pot

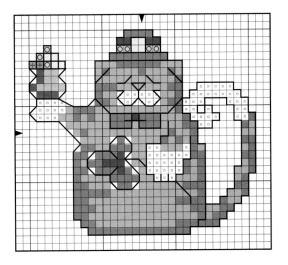

March 17

Design size: 42 wide x 18 high

	Anchor	DMC
▪	225	702
▪	228	700
▪	110	208

Backstitch:
228—"IRISH"
228 (2 strands)—stem
110 (2 strands)—"HONORARY"

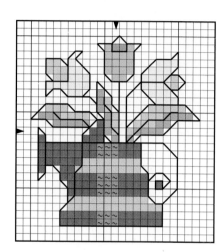

March 18

Design size: 23 wide x 25 high

	Anchor	DMC
▪	73	963
▪	75	962
▪	300	745
▪	311	3827
▪	1043	369
▪	241	966
~	875	3813
▪	876	3816

Backstitch:
211/562—leaves, stems, handle
401/413—flowers, can

March 19

Design size: 28 wide x 44 high

	Anchor	DMC
□	292	3078
▫	295	726
◇	297	973
▪	240	966
◉	243	703
~	387	712
▫	367	738
▪	1047	402

French Knot: 400/317
Backstitch:
244/702—leaves, stem
369/435—bulb, roots
1048/3776—flower
400—lettering

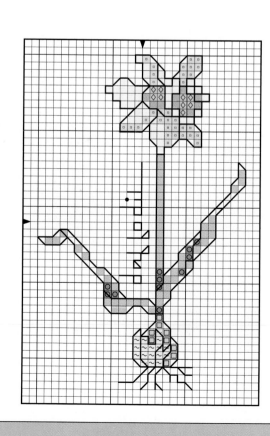

March 20

Design size: 24 wide x 27 high

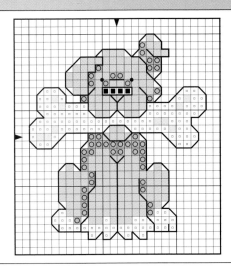

	Anchor	DMC
□	2	blanc
▨	361	738
◉	362/363	437/436
□	128	800
■	403	310

French Knots: 403
Backstitch:
349/301—dog (except nose & upper mouth)
400/317—bone
403—nose, upper mouth

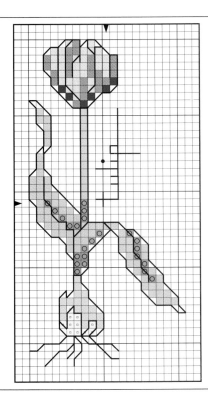

March 21

Design size: 21 wide x 43 high

	Anchor	DMC
□	103	211
▨	95/96	554/3608
▨	94	917
▨	241	966
◉	243	703
▫	387	712
□	367	738

French Knot: 400/317
Backstitch:
94—flower
244/702—leaves, stem
369/435—bulb, roots
400—lettering

March 22

Design size: 34 wide x 38 high

	Anchor	DMC
□	2	blanc
▨	74	3354
▨	96	3609
□	301	744
▨	302	743
~	206	564
▨	185	964
▨	130	809
□	881	945
▨	1047	402

French Knot: 403/310
Backstitch:
76/961—hearts
1001/976—moon
1049/3826—bear (except eyes & nose)
400/317—blanket, clothes
403—eyes, nose

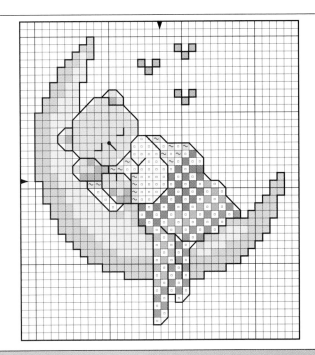

March 23

Design size: 21 wide x 29 high

	Anchor	DMC
▫	2	blanc
~	66	3688
▨	68	3687
▢	881	945
▨	1047	402
■	403	310

French Knot: 403
Backstitch:
1049/3826—bear (except eyes & nose)
400/317—shoes, skirt
403—bodice, eyes, nose

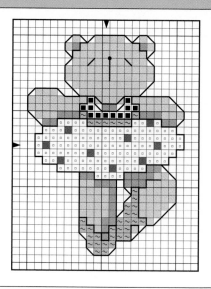

March 24

Design size: 23 wide x 25 high

	Anchor	DMC
▫	2	blanc
~	73	963
▨	334	606
▢	302	743
▢	240	966
◎	160	827
▨	145	809
▢	342	211
▫	2/234	blanc/762
▲	398	415
▨	235	414
■	403	310

French Knots: 403
Backstitch:
210/562—leaves
110/208—petals
349/301—flower center
236/3799—mouse, cat

March 25

Design size: 46 wide x 36 high

	Anchor	DMC
▫	2	blanc
■	334	606
▢	885	739
▨	891	676
■	403	310

French Knots: 403
Backstitch:
349/301—dog (except nose)
1048/3776—kite string
400/317—kite, kite tail
403—nose

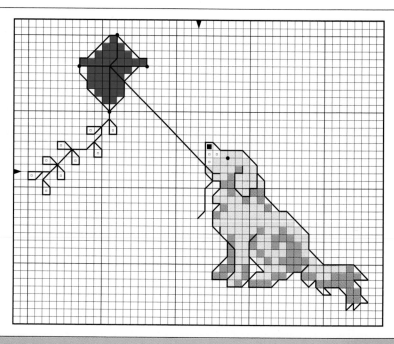

March 26

Design size: 11 wide x 33 high

	Anchor	DMC
▢	306	783
▢	240	966
▢	242	989
▨	226	703
■	403	310

Backstitch:
1005/816 (2 strands)—thread
211/562—hat, shamrocks
370/434—hat band

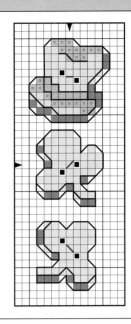

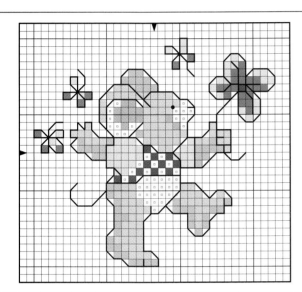

March 27

Design size: 33 wide x 30 high

	Anchor	DMC
▫	2	blanc
▢	23	3713
▢	1043/240	369/966
▨	226	703
▨	211	562
▢	366	951
▢	368	437

French Knot: 403/310
Backstitch:
211—shirt, shamrocks
371/434—mouse

March 28

Design size: 23 wide x 42 high

	Anchor	DMC
▫	2	blanc
▢	50	605
▨	52	957
⊞	225	702
▨	227	701
■	923	3818
⊙	1092	995
▢	1038/185	519/964
∼	1039/187	518/958
▨	169/189	806/943
▢	1012	754
▢	868	353

	Anchor	DMC
⌃	368	437
◬	369	435

Backstitch:
54/956—dress trim edge, roses
923—green edges of dress, leaves
1039—wings
169—gem, bottom edge of
　　skirt, "AQUAMARINE"
1013/3778—skin
370/434—hair
403/310—eyes

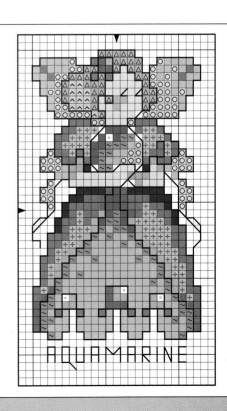

March 29

Design size: 18 wide x 30 high

	Anchor	DMC
■	333	608
□	301	744
□	302	743
▫	328	3341
□	875	3813
≈	342	211
■	109	209

Backstitch:
877/3815—leaves, stems
400/317—remaining outlines

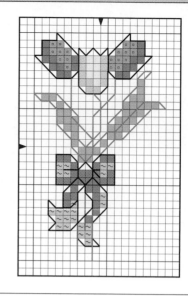

March 30

Design size: 37 wide x 28 high

	Anchor	DMC
□	23	3713
◎	36	3326
□	313	742
▫	206	564
▫	1092	995
∧	186	959
□	128	800
■	130	809
□	234	762
■	403	310

French Knots: 403
Backstitch:
895/223—pig (except eye & hooves)
210/562—grass
400/317—hooves, bird, tie
403—notes, eye, baton, vest

March 31

Design size: 52 wide x 35 high

	Anchor	DMC
▫	2	blanc
≈	128	800
□	9159	828
■	1039	518
□	881	945
□	369	435
□	398	415
■	403	310

French Knots: 403
Backstitch:
162/517—skirt stripes, rain,
   wind lines
1049/3826—bear
400/317—remaining clothes
403—umbrella, shoes

46

April

April 16

April 7

April 2

April 24

April 14

April 15

April 20

April 11

April 30

April 23

April 13

April 17

April 29

April 6

April 28

April 22

April 10

April 8

April 21

April 9

April 4

April 19

April 5

April 18

April 1

April 26

April 3

April 25

April 27

April 12

April 1

Design size: 23 wide x 21 high

French Knots:
925/971—"i" in "April"
187/958—"i" in "Bring"
Backstitch:
334/606—"Showers"
925—"April"
242/989—"Flowers"
187—"Bring May"

April 2

Design size: 28 wide x 29 high

	Anchor	DMC
·	2	blanc
	73	963
	50	605
	77/76	3687/961
	842	3013
⊙	843	3012
	845	730

Backstitch:
76—"Sweet Pea"
77—flowers
78/3685—"APRIL"
845—leaves, stem, tendril
360/898—border

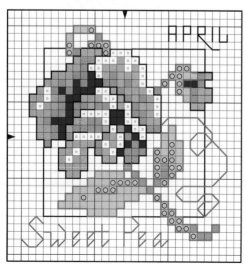

April 3

Design size: 28 wide x 19 high

	Anchor	DMC		Anchor	DMC
□	2	blanc		368	437
	73	963		370	434
~	75	962			
	240	966			
⊙	1092	995			
	1038	519			
	108	210			
	366	951			

French Knot: 403/310
Backstitch:
210/562—leaves
371/434—nest, branch, stems
400/317—bird, eggs

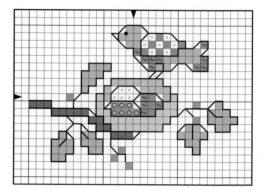

April 4

Design size: 28 wide x 26 high

	Anchor	DMC
·	2	blanc
~	48	3689
	38	961
■	39	309
□	300	745
⊠	311	3827
	1043	369
△	241	966
	120	3747
	342	211
⊙	109	209
	234	762

French Knots: 403/310
Backstitch:
39—flower (except center)
210/562—leaf, stem
1048/3776—flower center
400/317—mouse, butterfly (except body)
403—butterfly body

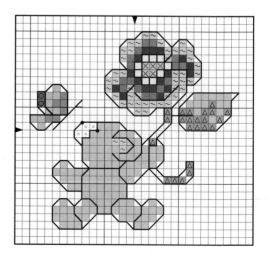

April 5

Design size: 21 wide x 28 high

Anchor	DMC		Anchor	DMC
~ 25	3326		◎ 1039	518
▨ 38	961		▨ 110	208
☐ 386	3823		◈ 358	801
▨ 943	422			
▨ 374	420			
▨ 205	912			
▨ 1038	519			

Backstitch:
358 (2 strands)—eyes
358—remaining
  outlines

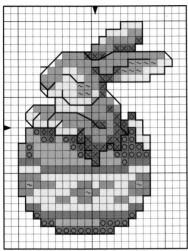

April 6

Design size: 28 wide x 30 high

Anchor	DMC	Backstitch:
☐ 50	605	1048/3776—yellow
▨ 57	602	egg
☐ 301	744	268—wreath
~ 302	743	187—turquoise eggs
☐ 259	772	110—purple eggs
▨ 265	3347	
▨ 268	469	
☐ 1092	995	
▨ 187	958	
☐ 108	210	
▨ 110	208	

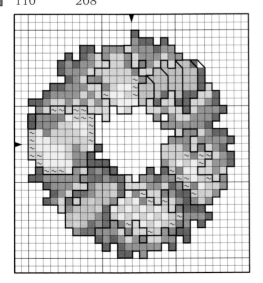

April 7

Design size: 21 wide x 23 high

Anchor	DMC	Backstitch:
∘ 2	blanc	**1024**—mouth
☐ 73	963	1013/3778—baby skin
☐ 1012	754	400/317—remaining
☐ 234	762	outlines

French Knots:
1024/3328—rabbit nose
403/310—eyes

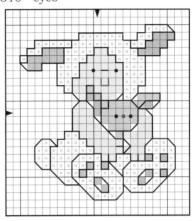

April 8

Design size: 25 wide x 38 high

Anchor	DMC	
∘ 2	blanc	**188**—word separations
▨ 891	676	1001—chick eyes
▨ 1001/1002	976/977	**Backstitch:**
~ 203	564	1001—"APRIL," basket,
▨ 187/188	958/3812	chicks
☐ 108	210	**188**—zigzag line under
▨ 111	553	bows

French Knots:
108—bows, chick
  separations

110/208—pot zigzag
  lines, bows,
  "BUNNIES," "CHICKS"

April 9

Design size: 37 wide x 34 high

	Anchor	DMC		Anchor	DMC
▫	2	blanc	▨	398	415
■	334	606	▨	235	414
■	1005	816	■	403	310
◎	96	3609			
▨	305	743			
∼	361	738			
▨	241	966			
▨	342	211			
▨	109	209			
▨	881	945			
▨	1047	402			
△	1048	3776			
■	370	434			

French Knot: 403
Backstitch:
334—broom straw line
1049/3826—bear
  (except nose)
370—mop & broom
  handles
403—nose
400/317—remaining
  outlines

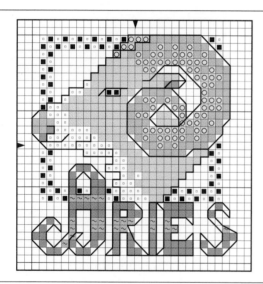

April 10

Design size: 28 wide x 29 high

	Anchor	DMC
▫	2	blanc
∼	1012	754
▨	338	922
▨	942	738
◎	933	543
▨	369	435
▨	231	453
▨	233	452
■	403	310

Backstitch: 403

April 11

Design size: 31 wide x 43 high

	Anchor	DMC
▫	2	blanc
■	334	606
▨	1070	993
∼	387	712
▨	388	3033
▨	378	841
▨	1086	839
◎	347	402
■	400	317

Backstitch:
400—bird house, cat (except eye),
  bird (except legs)
403/310—cat eye, bird legs

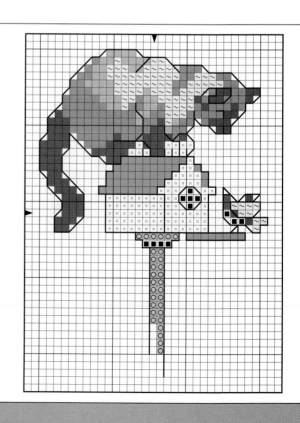

April 12

Design size: 31 wide x 30 high

	Anchor	DMC
▫	2	blanc
☐	50	605
▨	55	957
☐	386	3823
☐	311	3827
▨	265	3347
▨	1092	995
☐	342	211
▨	109	209

Backstitch: 400/317

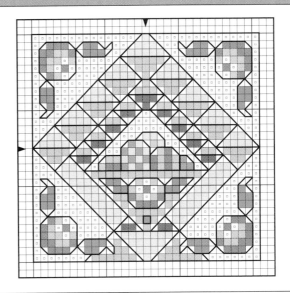

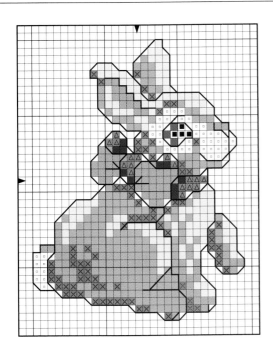

April 13

Design size: 29 wide x 37 high

	Anchor	DMC
▫	2	blanc
▨	24	963
▨	129	800
△	145	809
■	147	797
☐	885	739
▨	1047	402
☒	1048	3776
▨	355	975
■	403	310

Backstitch:
147—ribbon
403—eye, nose, muzzle
355—remaining rabbit

April 14

Design size: 32 wide x 34 high

	Anchor	DMC
▫	2	blanc
▨	85	3609
☐	292	3078
~	295	726
☐	206	564
△	208	563
☐	366	951
☐	368	437
☒	401	413

Backstitch:
210/562—bird house, leaves, stems, "SPRING"
370/434—house roofs
400/317—remaining outlines

April 15

Design size: 20 wide x 36 high

	Anchor	DMC			Anchor	DMC
▫	2	blanc		◎	366	951
⊠	74	3354		⊛	368	437
	1012	754		~	347	402
	868	353		▪	370	434
	301	744				
	302	743				
	208	563				
	129	809				
	342	211				
	109	209				

French Knots: 400/317
Backstitch:
111/553—hat
370—ribbon, skin
400—remaining outlines

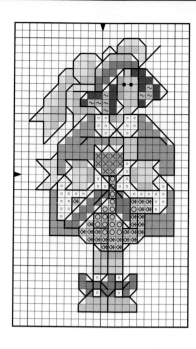

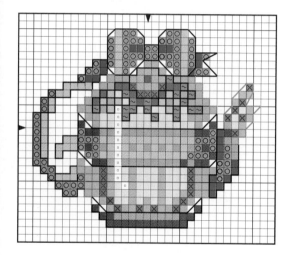

April 16

Design size: 31 wide x 26 high

	Anchor	DMC
▫	2	blanc
	23	3713
⊠	27	899
	29	309
	301	744
	306	783
~	265	3347
	267	469
	185	964
◎	187	958
	189	943
	108	210
	110	208

Backstitch:
29—pink flowers
267—leaves
189—bow, handle,
   turquoise part of spout
   & flowers
111/553—teapot middle
   & bottom, purple part
   of spout
1001/976—remaining
   teapot

April 17

Design size: 53 wide x 26 high

	Anchor	DMC
▫	2	blanc
	241	966
	885	739
	362	437
■	370	434
	388	3033
⊞	903	640
	234	762
	399	318
■	403	310

Backstitch:
210/562—leaves
370—branch, roots, bone
400/317—dog (except face)
403—face

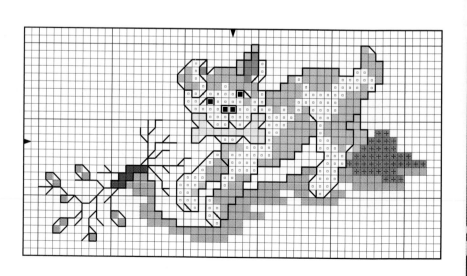

April 18

Design size: 14 wide x 39 high

	Anchor	DMC
□	2	blanc
▨	24	963
∼	313	742
▨	316	970
▨	240	966
△	226	703
□	128	800
■	403	310

French Knots: 403

Backstitch:
334/606 (2 strands)—buttonhole thread
370/434—inner rabbit ears, outer muzzle,
   carrot (except top)
403—inner muzzle, nose
400/317—remaining outlines

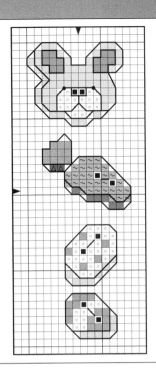

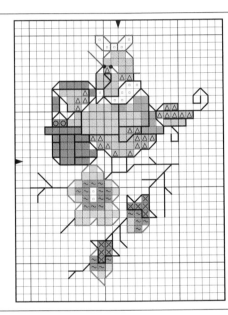

April 19

Design size: 24 wide x 33 high

	Anchor	DMC		Anchor	DMC
□	2	blanc	⊠	875	3813
□	23	3713	□	342	211
∼	25	3326			
◎	85	3609			
□	361	738			
△	362	437			
▨	1001	976			
□	1043	369			
▨	241	966			

French Knots: 400/317

Backstitch:
38/961—flowers
110/208—hat, bow
393/640—branches
400—remaining outlines

April 20

Design size: 27 wide x 34 high

	Anchor	DMC
□	2	blanc
∼	73	963
▨	50	605
◎	68	3687
□	293	727
▨	240	966
⊠	342	211
□	234	762
■	403	310

French Knots: 403

Backstitch:
210/562—leaves
1048/3776—flower, bow center
400/317—remaining outlines

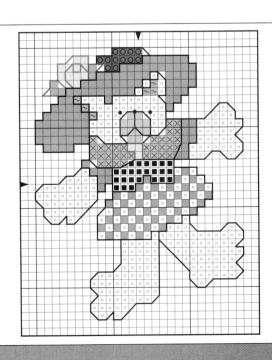

April 21

Design size: 26 wide x 36 high

Anchor	DMC
36	3326
38	961
305	743
304	741
311	3827
259	772
241	966
128	800
130	809
881	945
1047	402
403	310

French Knots: 403
Backstitch:
39/309—flower petals
244/702—leaves, stem
146/798—wings
1049/3826—bear, flower
  center, honey, bee
  bodies (except stripes)
403—antennae, hat,
  clothes, bee body
  stripes, honey pot

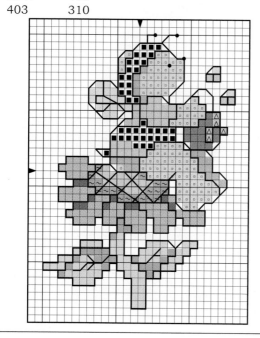

April 22

Design size: 34 wide x 28 high

Anchor	DMC
2	blanc
334	606
323	3825
240	966
128	800
403	310

French Knots: 403
Backstitch:
210/562—frog (except
  eye), grass
370/434—duck bill & feet
400/317—duck
403—frog eye, scarf

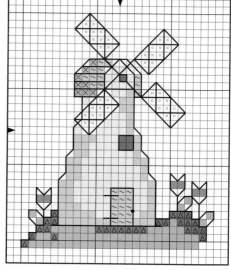

April 23

Design size: 26 wide x 31 high

Anchor	DMC	Anchor	DMC
2	blanc	369	435
85	3609	400	317
300	745		
311	3827		
240	966		
226	703		
368	437		

French Knot: 333/608
Backstitch:
333—blades, window,
  door (except hinges)
400—remaining outlines

April 24

Design size: 36 wide x 30 high

Anchor	DMC	Anchor	DMC
2	blanc	398	415
334	606	403	310
323	3825		
295	726		
206	564		
129	809		
146	798		
387	712		
881	945		
368	437		
1047	402		
1048	3776		

French Knots: 403
Backstitch:
210/562—leaves, grass
146—pant line
1049/3826—tree trunk
  & branches, nest,
  hat flower, bear
  (except nose)
400/317—clothes, eggs
403—hat, nose, bird

April 25

Design size: 20 wide x 29 high

	Anchor	DMC
	2	blanc
▨	334	606
☐	386	3823
∼	301	744
☐	302	743
▨	342	211

French Knots:
334—hat, coat
400/317—eye
Backstitch:
334—sleeve stripes
400—remaining outlines

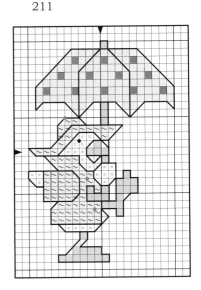

April 26

Design size: 20 wide x 32 high

	Anchor	DMC
	2	blanc
◎	74	3354
▨	95	554
☐	1012	754
☐	292	3078
▨	206	564
☐	128	800
▨	349	301

French Knots: 349
Backstitch:
1024/3328—mouth
1013/3778—skin
  (except nose)
146/798—raindrops
349—nose, hair
400/317—remaining
  outlines

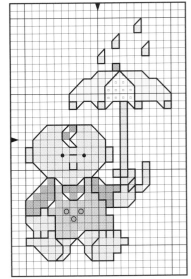

April 27

Design size: 44 wide x 42 high

	Anchor	DMC
▨	176	793
◎	177	792
▨	98	553
▨	111	208

Backstitch:
111 (2 strands)—center star
177 (2 strands)—center star
177—remaining outlines

April 28

Design size: 23 wide x 41 high

	Anchor	DMC
▫	2	blanc
♡	50	605
▫	1012	754
	868	353
^	311	3827
	1002	977
	266	3347
+	128	800
	130	809
~	131	798
	132	797
⊙	103	211
	96	3609
	99	552

Backstitch:
1001/976—hair, skin
268/469—leaves
130—wings
132—flower, dress, gem, "DIAMOND"
403/310—eyes

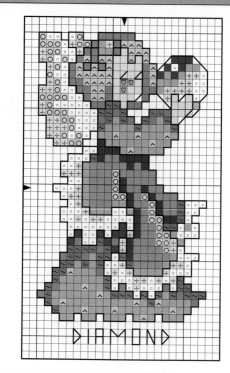

April 29

Design size: 32 wide x 22 high

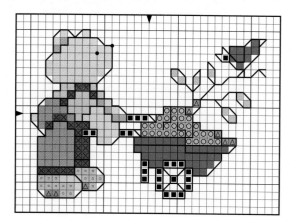

	Anchor	DMC		Anchor	DMC
	334	606	⊙	391	3033
	305	743	■	403	310
	206	564			
	129	809			
✕	131	798			
	881	945			
	1047	402			
⊙	347	3776			
△	349	301			

French Knots: 403
Backstitch:
210/562—leaves
349—bear, branch, dirt
400/317—clothes, shoes
403—bird, wheelbarrow

April 30

Design size: 29 wide x 38 high

	Anchor	DMC
	73	963
	76	961
	301/311	744/3827
	313	742
	1092	995
	186	959
	95	554
	97	553
■	400	317

French Knots: 355/975
Backstitch:
1074/992 (2 strands)—thread
355—thimble, lettering
400—remaining outlines

May 25

May 2

May 20

May 16

May 22

May 30

May 3

May 12

May 19

May 1

May 24

May 7

May 23

May 14

May 17

May 21

May

May 28

EMERALD

May 26

May 10

Taurus

May 15

May 8

MAY

BEES·BUZZ·BEES

May 4

May 5

May 31

May 18

May 9

May 27

May 11

May 6

I ♥ MOM

May 29

May 13

May 1

Design size: 26 wide x 28 high

	Anchor	DMC	Backstitch:
▫	2	blanc	210/562—leaves, stems
♡	50	605	400/317—flowers
▨	314	741	
▫	301	744	
◉	302	743	
▨	259	772	
△	241	966	
▨	342	211	

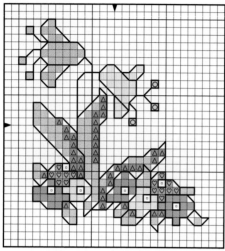

May 3

Design size: 19 wide x 30 high

	Anchor	DMC	French Knots: 403
▫	2	blanc	**Backstitch:**
▫	300	745	349/301—bears (except
▨	185	964	mom's nose), skirt
△	187	958	400/317—blanket,
▨	96	3609	apron, sleeves
▫	881	945	403—nose
▨	1047	402	
■	403	310	

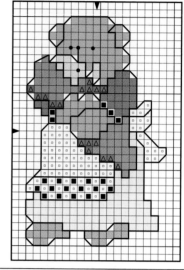

May 2

Design size: 28 wide x 30 high

	Anchor	DMC	French Knot: 121/809
▫	2	blanc	**Backstitch:**
▫	302	743	845—yellow-green
▫	259	772	stems & leaf
▨	842	3013	211—green leaf
▨	843	3012	121—"Lily of the Valley"
▨	845	730	110/208—flowers,
▫	206	564	border, "MAY"
▨	208	563	
■	211	562	
▫	2/120	blanc/3747	
▨	117	341	

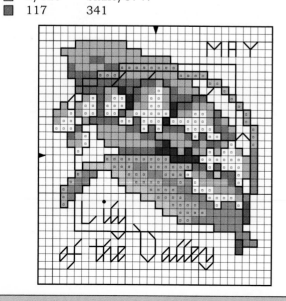

May 4

Design size: 26 wide x 30 high

	Anchor	DMC	French Knots: 403
▫	2	blanc	**Backstitch:**
▨	73	963	**210/562**—leaf, stem
♡	76	961	**1038/519**—cloud
~	1012	754	349/301—flower, sun,
⊠	337	3776	bear (except nose),
▫	301	744	giraffe
▨	240	966	403—nose
▨	120	3747	400/317—remaining
◉	367	738	outlines
▨	234	762	
■	403	310	

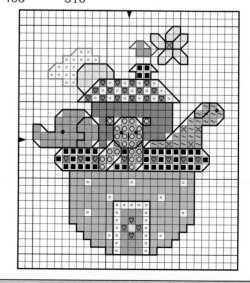

May 5

Design size: 17 wide x 30 high

Anchor	DMC
2	blanc
24	963
240	966
85	3609
336	758

French Knots: 403/310
Backstitch:
210/562—leaves, stem
884/356—pot
400/317—flower, bunny

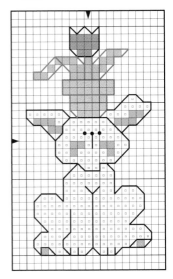

May 7

Design size: 28 wide x 16 high

Anchor	DMC
2	blanc
73	963
76	961
208	563
128	800
361	738
362	437
363	436

French Knot: 403/310
Backstitch:
365/435—rabbit
400/317—remaining outlines

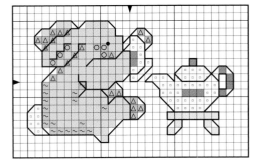

May 6

Design size: 30 wide x 28 high

Anchor	DMC
2	blanc
50	605
55	957
333	608
46	666
302	743
314	741
261	989
262	3363
185	964
1004	920

Backstitch:
46—pink flowers, lettering, heart
263/3362—green areas of wreath
188/3812—turquoise flowers
1004—yellow buds, butterfly (except antennae)
400/317—antennae

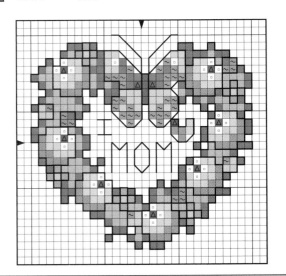

May 8

Design size: 25 wide x 38 high

Anchor	DMC
2	blanc
894	223
895	3722
896	3721
891	676
1001/1002	976/977
242/265	989/3347
244	702
1041	844
403	310

French Knots:
896—lettering separations
403—hive, bees
Backstitch:
896—zigzag lines
244—stems
244 (2 strands)— line over hive
1041—lettering
403—bees

May 9

Design size: 17 wide x 18 high

	Anchor	DMC
▫	2	blanc
◎	1021	761
▢	1012	754
▢	1092	995
◈	186	959
∼	391	3033

French Knots: 393/640
Backstitch:
1024/3328—mouth, bottle top
1013/3778—nose, skin
393—hair
400/317—shirt, diaper, bottle

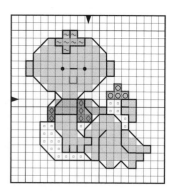

May 10

Design size: 27 wide x 38 high

	Anchor	DMC
▫	2	blanc
▢	1010	951
▢	1002	977
▢	1048	3776
▢	351	400
▢	260	772
◎	261	989
▢	876	3816

	Anchor	DMC
▢	231	453
▢	233	452
■	403	310

Backstitch:
876—border
403—remaining outlines

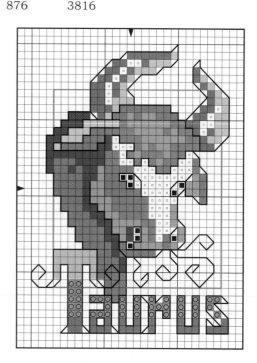

May 11

Design size: 24 wide x 24 high

	Anchor	DMC
▢	276	739
▢	293	727
▢	361	738
▫	362	437
▢	1043	369
▢	95	554
◎	97	553
▢	370	434
■	403	310

Backstitch:
210/562—leaves, stem
99/552—flower
370—dog (except eyes & nose), bee (except stripe)
403—eyes, nose, bee stripe

May 12

Design size: 30 wide x 30 high

	Anchor	DMC
▫	2	blanc
▢	386	3823
▢	48	3689
◎	50	605
▢	46	666
▢	129	809
▢	131	798
∼	342	211
■	403	310

Backstitch: 400/317

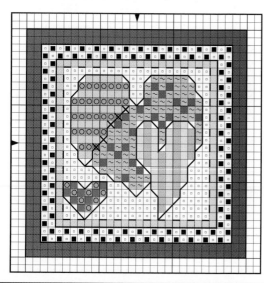

May 13

Design size: 22 wide x 26 high

	Anchor	DMC			Anchor	DMC
▫	2	blanc	⊠		161	813
▢	36	3326	▢		398	415
♡	76	961		**Backstitch:**		
▨	972	3803		972—flowers		
▨	265	3347		879—leaves		
△	243	703		161—"Mom," blue		
▨	879	500		flowers & stems		
▢	160 (1 strand)	827		400/317—cup,		
∼	160	827		lace		

May 14

Design size: 25 wide x 29 high

	Anchor	DMC
▫	2	blanc
♡	46	666
▨	1005	816
∼	329	3340
▨	332	946
▨	240	966
◎	243	703
▨	246	986
▢	347	402

Backstitch:
1005—cherries
246—leaves
352/300—branch, stems

May 15

Design size: 12 wide x 31 high

	Anchor	DMC			Anchor	DMC
▫	2	blanc	◎		368	437
▨	24	963	■		403	310
⊠	305	743		**French Knot:** 403		
▨	206	564		**Backstitch:**		
◣	209	913		27/899—flower		
∼	185	964		210/562—tree top, leaf		
▢	128	800		**370/434**—bird beak,		
▢	366	951		flower stem, nest		
				400/317—remaining outlines		

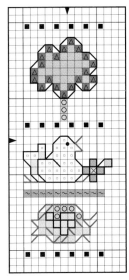

May 16

Design size: 33 wide x 34 high

	Anchor	DMC			Anchor	DMC
▫	2	blanc	▨		1002	977
▢	301	744	△		1048	3776
▢	185	964	▨		1004	920
◎	187	958	■		403	310
▨	189	943		**Backstitch:** 403		

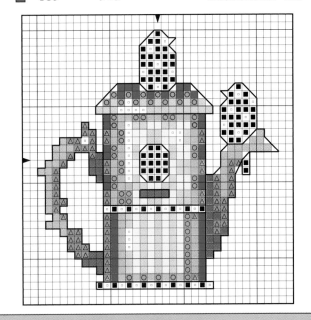

May 17

Design size: 32 wide x 32 high

	Anchor	DMC
□	2	blanc
▨	73	963
♡	75	962
□	301	744
▨	1092	995
◉	185/186	964/959
▨	96	3609
▨	2/234	blanc/762
▨	235	414

Backstitch:
76/961—bow
369/435—tassels
235—pillow
400/317—cat (except eye)
403/310—eye

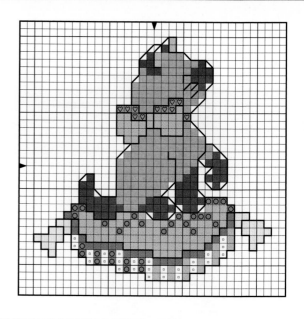

May 18

Design size: 28 wide x 34 high

	Anchor	DMC
□	2	blanc
□	387	712
▨	66	3688
~	336	758
◉	337/338	3776/922
▨	240	966
▨	928	3811
⊠	168	3810
□	342	211
▨	96	3609
□	881	945
▨	1047	402
■	403	310

French Knot: 403
Backstitch:
210/562—leaves, stems
98/553—shirt stripes
1049/3826—bear (except nose)
400/317—flower, pot, shirt, shorts
403—nose

May 19

Design size: 57 wide x 18 high

	Anchor	DMC
□	2	blanc
▨	74	3354
~	8	3824
□	301	744
▨	240	966

Backstitch:
77/3687—lettering
210/562—leaves, stems
130/809—flower petals
349/301—flower centers

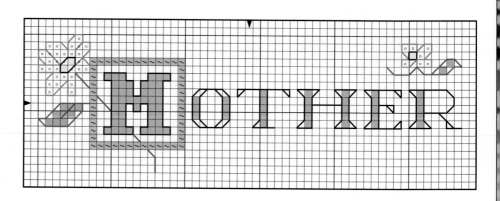

May 20

Design size: 19 wide x 30 high

	Anchor	DMC
■	334	606
□	328	3341
□	301	744
□	206	564
◩	208	563
□	128	800
◎	129	809

French Knots:
334—buttons
403/310—eye

Backstitch:
334—sleeve stripes
217/561—leaves
146/798—bird (except beak)
400/317—remaining outlines

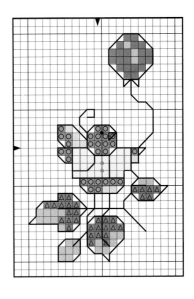

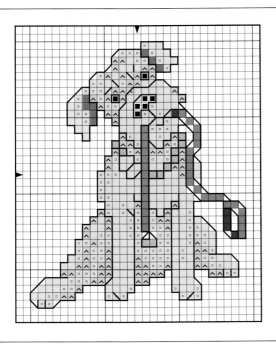

May 21

Design size: 29 wide x 35 high

	Anchor	DMC
□	276	739
■	334	606
■	1005	816
▫	367	738
⌃	369	435
■	358	801
■	234	762
■	403	310

Backstitch:
358—dog (except eyes & nose)
400/317—collar, leash
403—eyes, nose

May 22

Design size: 28 wide x 34 high

	Anchor	DMC
∼	23	3713
■	26	894
♡	28	892
□	842	3013
■	843	3012
⊠	845	730
■	240	966
■	243	703
◎	246	986
■	1044	895
■	875	3813
◬	877	3815

Backstitch:
28—flowers
845—base of flowers, peapod tops
1044—remaining outlines

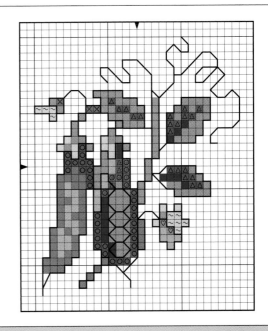

May 23

Design size: 33 wide x 24 high

	Anchor	DMC
☐	85	3609
◉	87	3607
■	94	917
☐	259	772
～	264	3348
▨	267	469
△	268	937

Backstitch:
102/550—cabbage
268—leaves

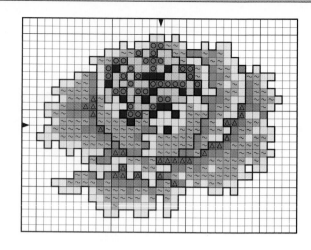

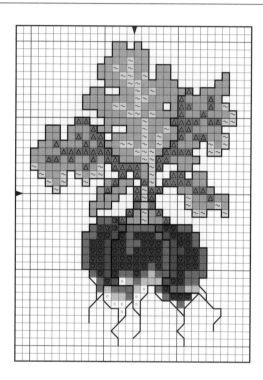

May 24

Design size: 28 wide x 40 high

	Anchor	DMC
▫	2	blanc
☐	49	3689
▨	38	961
♥	19	304
■	22	814
☐	311	3827
～	259	772
▨	265	3347
△	267	469
■	1003	922

Backstitch:
22—radishes
268/937—leaves
1003—rubber band

May 25

Design size: 30 wide x 33 high

	Anchor	DMC		Anchor	DMC
▫	2	blanc	▨	1039	518
■	334	606	☐	361	738
☐	1012	754	⊠	362	437
～	868	353			
◉	336	758			
☐	313	742			
☐	295	726			
+	300	745			
△	311	3827			
☐	206	564			
■	210	562			
☐	9159	828			

French Knots:
903/640—dirt
400/317—eyes
Backstitch:
217/561—watering
    can, leaves, stems
400—remaining
    outlines

May 26

Design size: 16 wide x 40 high

	Anchor	DMC
	2	blanc
◉	334	606
	313	742
	314	741
	305	743
	240	966
△	243	703
	128	800
	96	3609
■	403	310

Backstitch:
334 (2 strands)—flower & cloud thread
211/562—leaves
211 (2 strands)—rainbow thread
349/301—remaining flower & sun
400/317—remaining cloud & rainbow
403—buttonholes

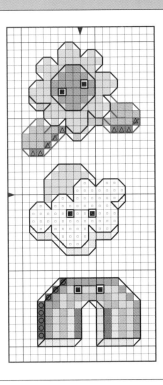

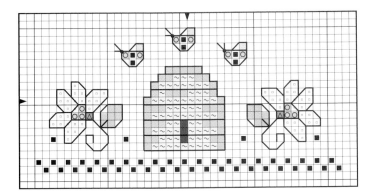

May 27

Design size: 42 wide x 19 high

	Anchor	DMC
	2	blanc
~	885	739
◉	305	743
	311	3827
	1043	369
△	241	966
	128	800
	370	434
■	403	310

French Knots: 403
Backstitch:
210/562—base of
   flowers, leaves,
   stems
369/435—bee bodies,
   hive, flower centers
235/414—wings,
   flower petals
403—antennae

May 28

Design size: 24 wide x 41 high

	Anchor	DMC
	2	blanc
	50	605
	1012	754
~	868	353
	1043	369
╱	225	702
	229	910
	923	3818
△	185	964
+	187	958
	130	809
	131	798
◉	342	211
	109	209
	111	553
	1048	3776
	1004	920

Backstitch:
225—wings
923—hair clip gem,
   green areas of dress,
   "EMERALD"
111—purple areas of
   dress
1048—skin
351/400—hair
403/310—eyes

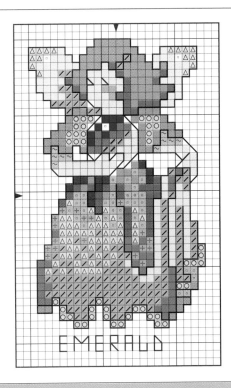

May 29

Design size: 31 wide x 31 high

	Anchor	DMC
▫	2	blanc
◼	334	606
◻	305	743
◻	128	800
◻	234	762
⊙	399	318
■	403	310

French Knot: 403
Backstitch:
371/434—yellow part of bird & legs
400/317—remaining outlines

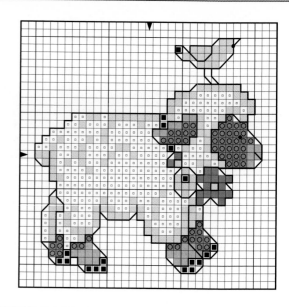

May 30

Design size: 31 wide x 31 high

	Anchor	DMC
▫	2	blanc
◻	48	3689
♡	50	605
∼	1012	754
⊙	313	742
⊞	300	745
◻	891	676
◻	120	3747
◻	234	762

French Knots: 54/956
Backstitch:
136/799—dress stripes
235/414—remaining outlines

May 31

Design size: 47 wide x 35 high

	Anchor	DMC
▫	2	blanc
◻	206	564
⊙	1092	995
▲	120	3747
◻	85	3609
◻	881	945
◻	349	301
■	403	310

French Knots: 403
Backstitch:
210/562—leaves, stems,
   tendrils
349—bear, shoes
400/317—remaining
   outlines

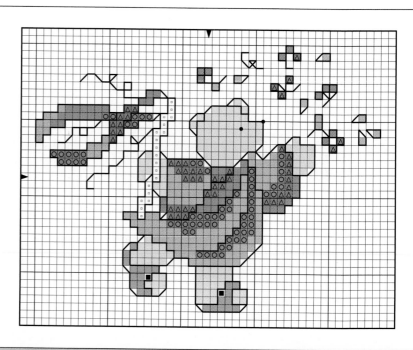

June

June 2

June 1

June 6

June 16

June 11

June 24

June 5

June 22

June 12

June 18

June 19

June 13

June 15

June 26

June 25

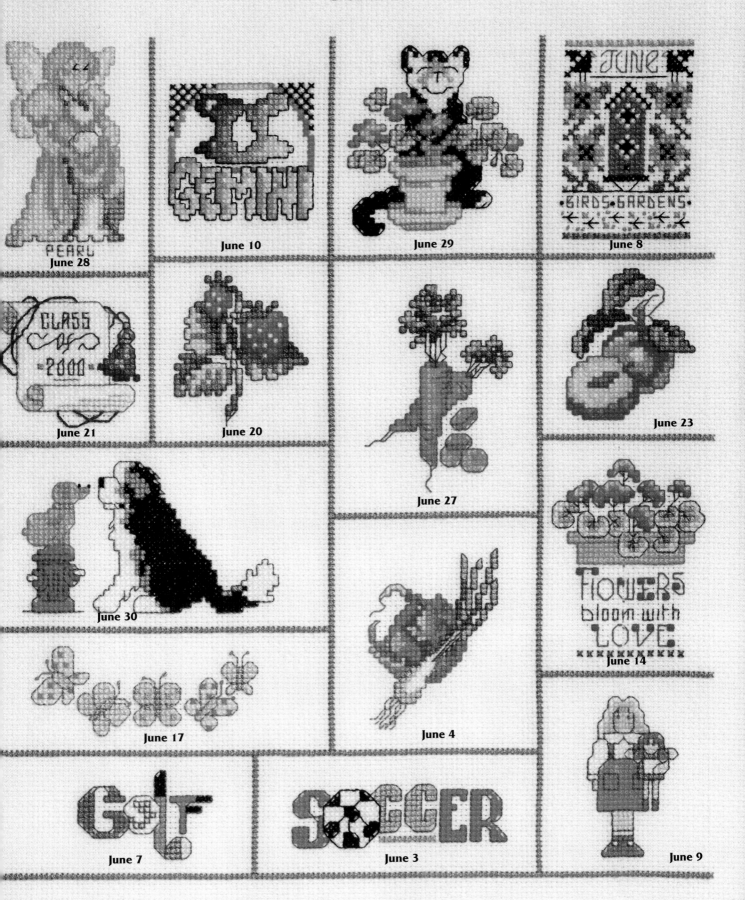

June 28

June 10

June 29

June 8

June 21

June 20

June 27

June 23

June 30

June 14

June 17

June 4

June 7

June 3

June 9

June 1

Design size: 22 wide x 20 high
Note: For diaper pin use 25 for girl, 167 for boy.

	Anchor	DMC	Backstitch:
▫	2	blanc	370/434—bear (except
▪	25	3326	face)
⊙	8	3824	382/3371—mouth
▪	167	519	382 (2 strands)—eyes, nose
▪	366	951	400/317—diaper, pin head
~	368	437	400 (2 strands)—remaining
▪	234	762	pin

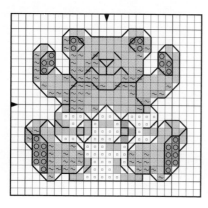

June 2

Design size: 28 wide x 30 high

	Anchor	DMC	Backstitch:
⊙	9046	321	9046—"JUNE"
▪	1005	816	1005—flower (except
▪	328	3341	center), border
▪	333	608	333—"Rose"
▫	300	745	246—leaves, stems
△	302	743	1049/3826—flower
▪	259	772	center
▪	265	3347	
~	257	905	
▪	246	986	

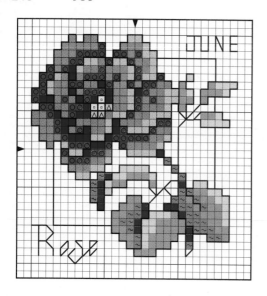

June 3

Design size: 42 wide x 12 high

	Anchor	DMC
▫	2	blanc
▪	334	606
▪	225	702
▪	129	809
▪	403	310

Backstitch:
400/317—letters
403—ball

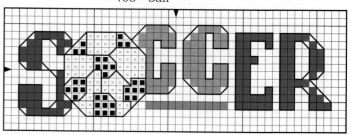

June 4

Design size: 25 wide x 35 high

	Anchor	DMC
▫	2	blanc
▪	85	3609
▽	87	3607
▪	1029	915
▪	259	772
~	265	3347
△	267	469
⊗	268	937
▪	361	738
⊙	1001	976
✕	1049	3826
▪	231	453

Backstitch:
1029—purple portion of Bermuda onion
268—green onion top
1049—Bermuda onion skin
233/452—remaining outlines

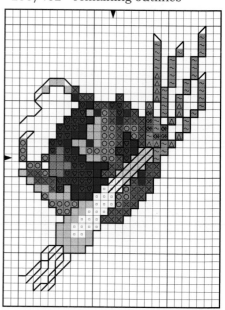

74

June 5

Design size: 24 wide x 24 high

	Anchor	DMC
▫	2	blanc
☐	301	744
◉	306	783
☐	160	827
~	1039	518
☒	162	517

Backstitch:
162—can (except heart, spout, & bottom edge)
349/301—remaining outlines

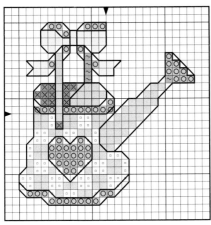

June 6

Design size: 34 wide x 31 high

	Anchor	DMC
▫	2	blanc
☐	48	3689
☐	50	605
♡	57	602
☐	301	744
☐	302	743
☐	314	741
△	1001	976
☐	265	3347
☐	268	469
☐	120	3747

French Knots: 403/310
Backstitch:
57—heart
1001—rings, gold area
  of wreath
268—remaining wreath
400/317—birds (except
  beaks)
403—beaks, string

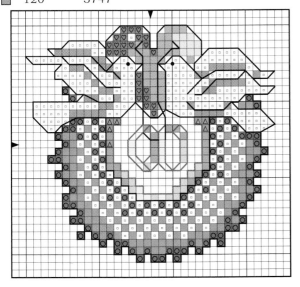

June 7

Design size: 26 wide x 17 high

	Anchor	DMC
▫	2	blanc
▨	334	606
▨	227	701
▨	1048	3776
☐	2/234	blanc/762
◉	399	318
■	403	310

Backstitch: 400/317

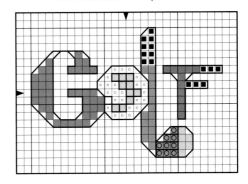

June 8

Design size: 25 wide x 38 high

	Anchor	DMC
▫	2	blanc
▨	896	3721
☐	891	676
▨	1001/1002	976/977
~	266	3347
▨	211	562
■	403	310

Backstitch:
896—lettering
1001—bird beaks
403—remaining
  outlines

French Knots:
1001—seeds by tracks
403—lettering separations

June 9

Design size: 18 wide x 31 high

	Anchor	DMC
□	2	blanc
♡	26	894
■	33	3706
□	1012	754
~	868	353
□	300	745
◎	311	3827
■	168	3810
⊠	349	301
■	400	317

French Knots: 400
Backstitch: 400

June 10

Design size: 28 wide x 26 high

	Anchor	DMC		Anchor	DMC
□	2	blanc	■	129	809
■	334	606	■	146	798
□	300	745	■	148	312
~	311	3827	■	403	310
□	302	743			
◎	316	970			
△	1003	922			
□	128	800			

Backstitch:
334—arch
403—remaining
    outlines

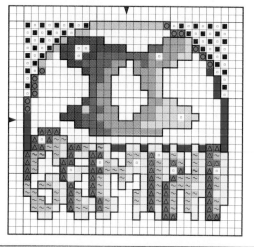

June 11

Design size: 23 wide x 20 high

	Anchor	DMC
□	2	blanc
■	334	606
□	300	745
⊠	311	3827
■	209	913
~	9159	828
	129	809
△	136	799
	342	211
■	109	209
□	398	415

French Knots: 403/310
Backstitch:
161/813—dress, veil
400/317—remaining
    outlines

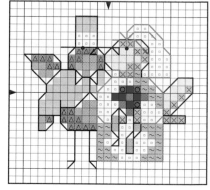

June 12

Design size: 30 wide x 30 high

	Anchor	DMC
□	2	blanc
□	386	3823
	85	3609
■	87	3607
◎	109	209
	128	800
	130	809
△	131	798

Backstitch:
210/562—stem
400/317—remaining outlines

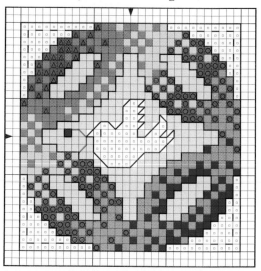

June 13

Design size: 29 wide x 20 high

Anchor	DMC	French Knots:
■ 334	606	370/434—dirt
□ 293	727	403/310—eye
▨ 1042	504	**Backstitch:**
◎ 215	320	162/517—bird (except
▨ 9159	828	beak & legs)
▲ 1038/1039	519/518	370—dirt
▨ 366	951	400/317—remaining
~ 368	437	outlines

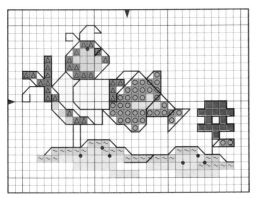

June 15

Design size: 19 wide x 19 high

Anchor	DMC	French Knots: 403/310
∘ 2	blanc	**Backstitch:**
▽ 74	3354	76/961—flowers
◉ 96	3609	**1024/3328**—mouth
□ 1012	754	1013/3778—skin (except
□ 301	744	nose)
⊠ 302	743	349/301—nose, hat
▨ 225	702	400/317—ball, clothes,
▨ 120	3747	diaper

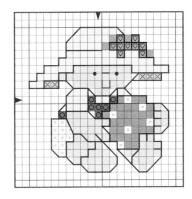

June 14

Design size: 30 wide x 38 high

Anchor	DMC	Backstitch:
■ 1005	816	1005—flowers,
∘ 313	742	"Flowers," "LOVE"
▨ 333	608	211—stems, leaves,
□ 259	772	remaining lettering
▲ 265	3347	884/356—pot
▨ 211	562	
~ 336	758	

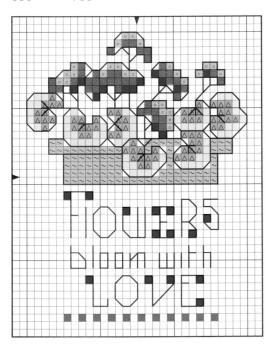

June 16

Design size: 29 wide x 35 high

Anchor	DMC	Backstitch:
∘ 2	blanc	43/814—lid, flowers
▨ 50	605	211/562—leaves,
▨ 57	602	stems, teapot spout
■ 59	326	& handle
□ 259	772	131/798—remaining
▨ 261	989	teapot
◎ 206	564	
▲ 208	563	
▨ 210	562	
▨ 928	3811	
▨ 130	809	

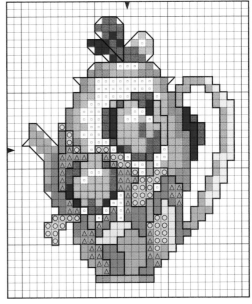

June 17

Design size: 44 wide x 17 high

	Anchor	DMC
■	334	606
▫	301	744
~	311	3827
◎	313	742
■	928	3811
▲	175	809
■	108	210

French Knots:
334—first & fourth butterfly
176/793—remaining butterflies

Backstitch:
334—first & fourth butterfly antennae
176—second & fifth butterfly antennae, third butterfly
903/640—remaining outlines

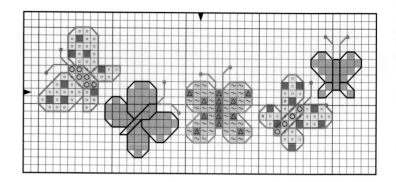

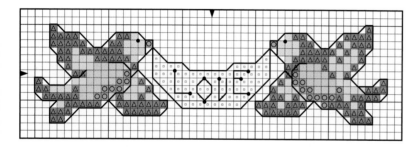

June 18

Design size: 48 wide x 13 high

	Anchor	DMC
▫	2	blanc
■	6/8	754/3824
◎	9	352
■	128	800
▲	160	827

French Knots:
978/312—lettering
403/310—eyes

Backstitch:
978—birds (except beaks & breasts), lettering
349/301—remaining outlines

June 19

Design size: 37 wide x 25 high

	Anchor	DMC
▫	2	blanc
■	334	606
■	85	3609
■	305	743
■	206	564
~	885	739
◎	362	437
☒	349	301
■	403	310

French Knots:
334—tulips
403—bee, hive

Backstitch:
210/562—leaves, stems, ground
401/413—remaining outlines

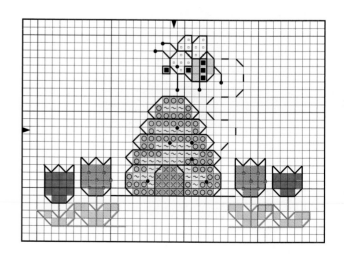

June 20

Design size: 26 wide x 30 high

	Anchor	DMC
▫	2	blanc
⊙	33	3706
	29	309
	1005	816
	259	772
△	266	3347
	268	469

Backstitch:
1005—berries
268—leaves, stem

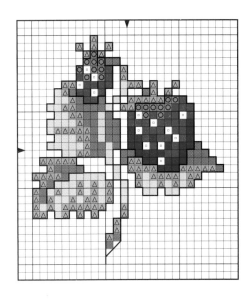

June 21

Design size: 28 wide x 25 high

	Anchor	DMC
▫	2	blanc
	361	738
⊙	943	422
✕	375	869
	129	809
∼	131	798
	133	820

Backstitch:
943—bottom three scroll lines
375—remaining scroll (except lettering)
133—tassel, lettering
133 (2 strands)—cord

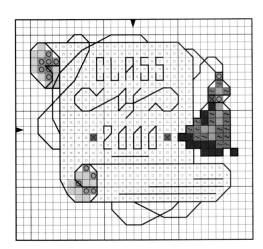

June 22

Design size: 36 wide x 26 high

	Anchor	DMC
▫	2	blanc
☐	300	745
∼	311	3827
☐	259	772
⊙	261	989
	1092	995
△	185	964
	109	209
	378	841
☐	398	415

Backstitch:
379/840—roof
400/317—remaining outlines

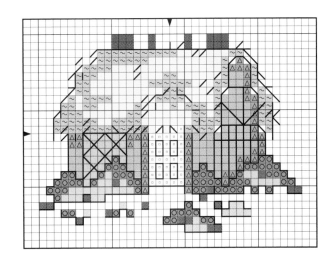

June 23

Design size: 25 wide x 29 high

	Anchor	DMC
⊡	1011	948
▨	9	352
▩	11	351
■	1005	816
▢	301	744
▨	302	743
▨	240	966
▨	243	703
■	246	986
~	347	402
⊚	349	301
■	351	400

Backstitch:
1005—peaches
246—leaves
351—stems

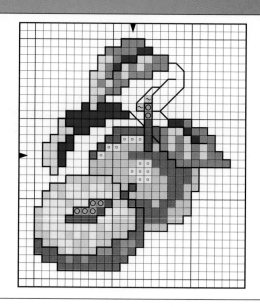

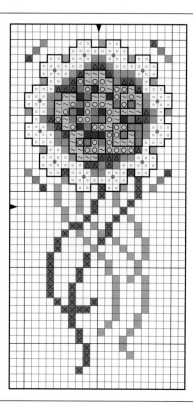

June 24

Design size: 20 wide x 44 high

	Anchor	DMC
▫	2	blanc
~	1011	948
⊚	24	963
▨	76	961
■	972	3803
▨	208	563
▲	217	561
▨	117	341
⊠	176	793

French Knots: 176
Backstitch:
972—flowers
176—lace

June 25

Design size: 31 wide x 31 high

	Anchor	DMC
▫	2	blanc
~	305	743
▢	885	739
⊚	891	676
▨	1043	369
▲	241	966
▨	881	945
▨	1047	402
⊠	349	301

French Knots: 403/310
Backstitch:
210/562—leaves, stems
349—bear (except nose),
  flower centers, bee
  body outlines &
  antennae, hive
399/318—flowers, bee
  wings
403—nose, bee body
  stripes

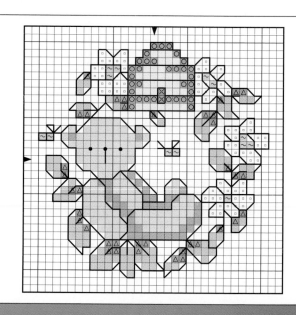

June 26

Design size: 33 wide x 27 high

Anchor	DMC
2	blanc
73	963
334	606
891	676
240	966
210	562
129	809
146	798
367	738
1047	402

Anchor	DMC
1048	3776
403	310

French Knots: 403
Backstitch:
76/961—pig, flamingo
(except beak & legs)
355/975—rabbit
400/317—remaining
outlines

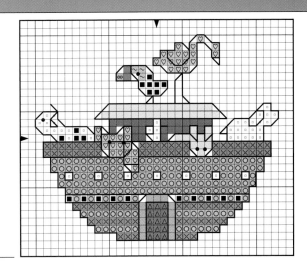

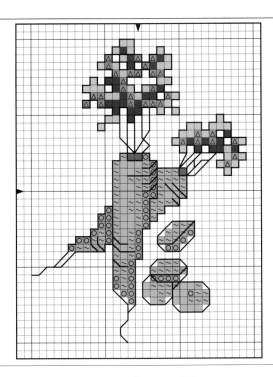

June 27

Design size: 29 wide x 40 high

Anchor	DMC
314	741
925	971
326	720
351	400
240	966
243	703
246	986

Backstitch:
351—carrots
246—carrot tops

June 28

Design size: 23 wide x 41 high

Anchor	DMC
2	blanc
48	3689
50	605
52	957
1012	754
868	353
311	3827
1002	977
259	772
265	3347
1031	3753
343	3752
921	931

Backstitch:
54/956—pink areas of dress
265—wings
267/469—green areas of dress
921—remaining dress, gem, "PEARL"
1001/976—hair, skin
403/310—eyes

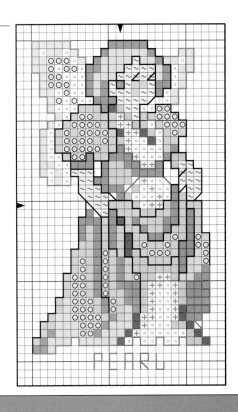

June 29

Design size: 34 wide x 36 high

	Anchor	DMC
▫	2	blanc
▨	1012	754
~	9575	3830
◎	313	742
▨	332	946
⊠	362	437
▨	1043	369
△	214	368
▣	1047	402
▨	884	356
■	403	310

Backstitch:
211/562—leaves, leaf stems
370/434—flowers, plant trunk
884—pot
403—cat

June 30

Design size: 50 wide x 29 high

	Anchor	DMC
▫	2	blanc
▨	334	606
▨	1006	304
▨	129	809
▨	1047	402
⊠	1048	3776
▨	399	318
■	403	310

French Knots: 403
Backstitch:
884/356—small dog
400/317—remaining outlines

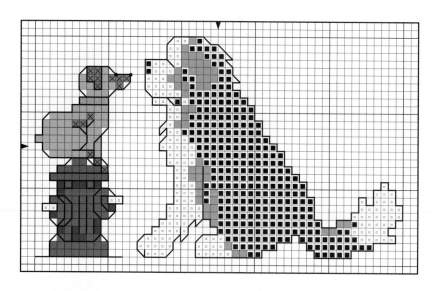

July

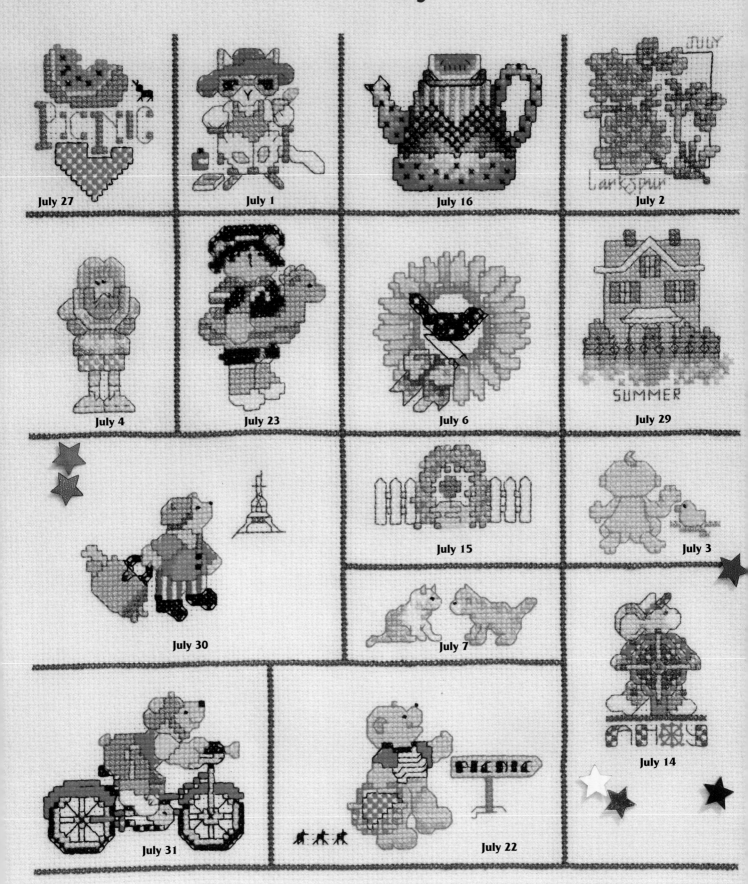

July 27

July 1

July 16

July 2

July 4

July 23

July 6

July 29

July 30

July 15

July 3

July 7

July 14

July 31

July 22

84

July

July 28

July 26

July 10

July 8

July 5

July 20

July 24

July 25

July 17

July 13

July 11

July 21

July 12

July 18

July 19

July 9

July 1

Design size: 26 wide x 27 high

Anchor	DMC
2	blanc
24	963
334	606
1006	304
96	3609
295	726
241	966
1031	3753
1039	518
403	310

Backstitch:
369/435—lemon,
lemonade line
403—nose
400/317—remaining
outlines

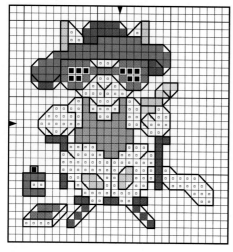

July 2

Design size: 28 wide x 30 high

Anchor	DMC
302	743
1003	922
842	3013
843	3012
845	730
120	3747
121	809
109	209

Backstitch:
1004/920—flower
centers
845—leaves, stems
121—"Larkspur"
122/3807—flowers
123/820—border
109—"JULY"

July 3

Design size: 26 wide x 20 high

Anchor	DMC
1012	754
323	3825
295	726
129	809
347	402

French Knot: 403/310
Backstitch:
1013/3778—skin
349/301—hair, duck

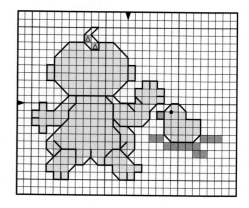

July 4

Design size: 16 wide x 30 high

Anchor	DMC	Anchor	DMC
2	blanc	881	945
1012	754	1047	402
868	353		
9	352		
323	3825		
301	744		
259	772		
241	966		
128	800		
129	809		

French Knots:
400/317
Backstitch:
1084/840—hair, skin
400—remaining
outlines

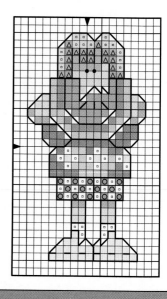

July 5

Design size: 27 wide x 23 high

Anchor	DMC		Anchor	DMC
96	3609		347	402
240	966		349	301
243	703		351	400
246	986		**Backstitch:**	
117	341		246—leaves	
142	798		112/552—plum	
178	791		351—branch, stems	

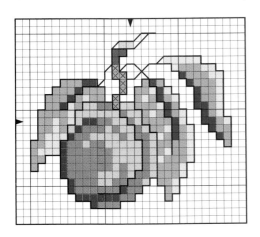

July 6

Design size: 31 wide x 31 high

Anchor	DMC		
2	blanc	**Backstitch:** 403	
314	741	**Backstitch:**	
301	744	132—bow	
302	743	**1049/3826**—wreath	
1001	976		
128	800		
130	809		
132	797		
403	310		

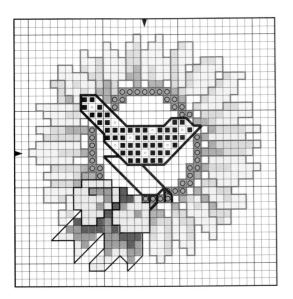

July 7

Design size: 34 wide x 12 high

Anchor	DMC
2	blanc
881	945
1047	402

French Knots: 403/310
Backstitch: 1049/3826

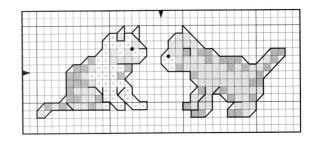

July 8

Design size: 25 wide x 38 high

Anchor	DMC	French Knots:
2	blanc	2 (2 strands)—flag
66	3688	**77**—word separations
77	3687	**Backstitch:**
334	606	**77**—"PICNICS,"
205	912	"PICNICS"
137	798	137—"JULY"
362	437	358—pie, basket, corn
369	435	403—seeds, zigzag
358	801	line, ants
403	310	

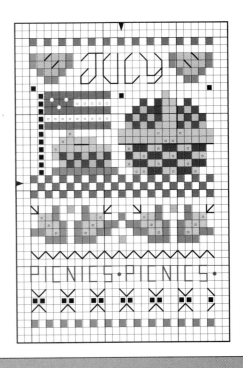

July 9

Design size: 25 wide x 21 high

	Anchor	DMC
▫	2	blanc
▨	73/74	963/3354
▨	66	3688
▨	68	3687
▨	259	772
◉	241	966

French Knots: 68
Backstitch:
68—berry outline
210/562—leaves
403/310—eyes
400/317—remaining
 outlines

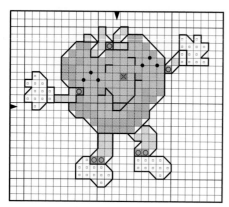

July 10

Design size: 33 wide x 29 high

	Anchor	DMC
▫	2	blanc
▨	6	754
▨	9	352
▨	11	351
▨	259	772
▨	260	3364
▨	876	3816
■	403	310

Backstitch: 403

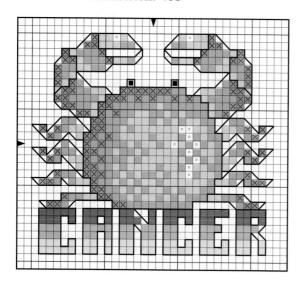

July 11

Design size: 37 wide x 24 high

	Anchor	DMC
▫	2	blanc
▨	24	963
▨	334	606
▨	295	726
▨	241	966
▨	129	809
▨	366	951
▨	368	437
■	403	310

French Knot: 403
Backstitch:
210/562—leaves, stem
146/798—sleeve stripes,
 water
371/434—mouse, dirt
400/317—remaining
 outlines

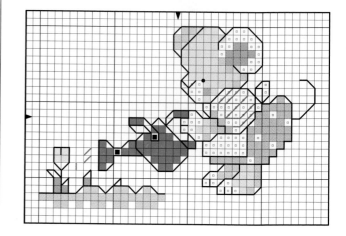

July 12

Design size: 30 wide x 30 high

	Anchor	DMC
▫	2	blanc
▨	329	3340
▨	300	745
◉	301/302	744/743
▨	313	742
▨	128	800
▨	130	809

Backstitch: 400/317

July 13

Design size: 10 wide x 28 high

Anchor	DMC	
■ 334	606	**French Knots:** 403
▫ 1043/240	369/966	**Backstitch:**
■ 226	703	2/blanc (2 strands)—thread
■ 399	318	211/562—watermelon
■ 403	310	button (except seeds)
		403—remaining outlines

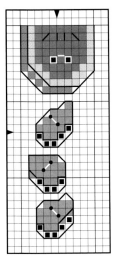

July 14

Design size: 20 wide x 30 high

Anchor	DMC	
▫ 2	blanc	**French Knots:**
◉ 23	3713	**334**—"O"
■ 334	606	**162**—eye
■ 129	809	**Backstitch:**
■ 162	517	**334**—"O"
□ 881	945	162—hat, remaining
■ 1048	3776	letters
□ 234	762	400—remaining outlines
~ 399	318	
△ 400	317	

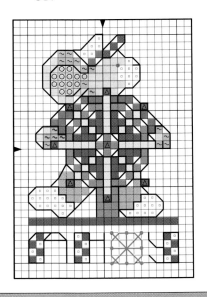

July 15

Design size: 31 wide x 16 high

Anchor	DMC	Backstitch:
▫ 2	blanc	76—flowers
▨ 73	963	210/562—leaves, grass
■ 76	961	1049/3826—path, trunk
▫ 1043	369	400/317—fence
▫ 240	966	
◎ 241	704	
■ 209	913	
□ 128	800	

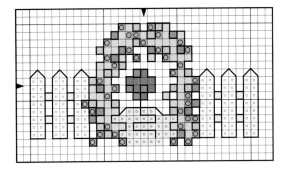

July 16

Design size: 35 wide x 26 high

Anchor	DMC
▫ 2	blanc
▨ 23	3713
♡ 27	899
■ 46	666
▨ 264	3348
△ 257	905
■ 246	986
□ 128	800
▨ 129	809
■ 131	798
◎ 133	820
■ 403	310

Backstitch:
246—watermelon lid
(except seeds)
403—remaining outlines

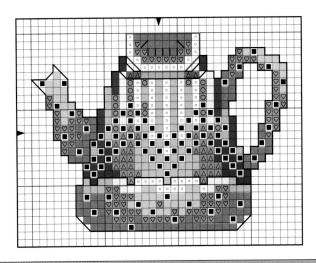

July 17

Design size: 46 wide x 18 high

	Anchor	DMC
▫	2	blanc
▨	73	963
▫	300	745
▨	1043	369
▨	928	3811
▨	347	402

French Knots: 400/317
Backstitch:
161/813—letters
400—remaining outlines

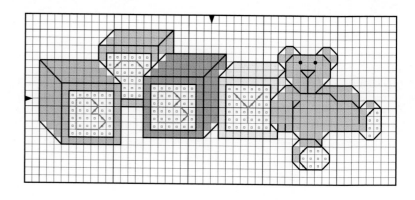

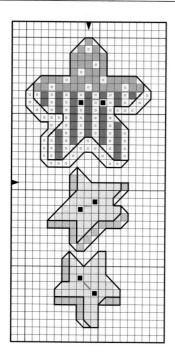

July 18

Design size: 17 wide x 38 high

	Anchor	DMC
▫	2	blanc
▨	334	606
▫	305	743
▨	306	783
▨	130	809
■	403	310

Backstitch:
146/798—flag line
146 (2 strands)—buttonhole thread
370/434—remaining star buttons
400/317—remaining flag button

July 19

Design size: 19 wide x 39 high

	Anchor	DMC
▫	2	blanc
▨	6	754
≈	9	352
▨	11	351
▨	240	966
▨	876	3816
▨	108	210
▨	379	840

French Knots:
876—"FRESH"
110/208—"Peach"
Backstitch:
876—"FRESH," leaf
110—"Peach," "P," "E"
379—peach, "I"

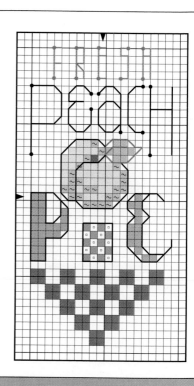

July 20

Design size: 22 wide x 32 high

Anchor	DMC
842	3013
843	3012
845	730
846	3011
97	554
87	3607

Backstitch:
846—artichoke leaves
99/552—top

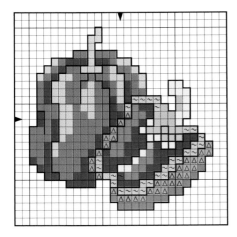

July 21

Design size: 25 wide x 24 high

Anchor	DMC
332	946
46	666
1005	816
323	3825
301	744
307	783
254/238	3348/703
227	701
923	3818

Backstitch:
1005—red pepper
923—green pepper

July 22

Design size: 49 wide x 29 high

Anchor	DMC
2	blanc
334	606
881	945
1047	402
366	951
369	435
403	310

French Knots: 403
Backstitch:
1049/3826—bear, basket, dirt,
   sign & post outlines
403—shirt, cloth, lettering, ants

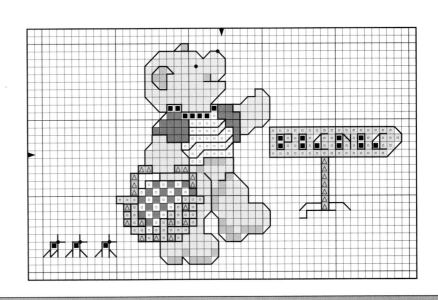

July 23

Design size: 25 wide x 36 high

	Anchor	DMC
□	2	blanc
▨	74	3354
□	240	966
▨	226	703
□	881	945
□	398	415
▨	235	414
■	403	310

French Knots: 403
Backstitch:
210/562—float (except mane)
1049/3826—bear (except nose)
400/317—clothes, mane
403—nose

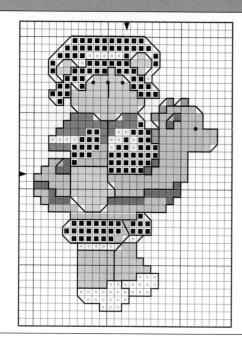

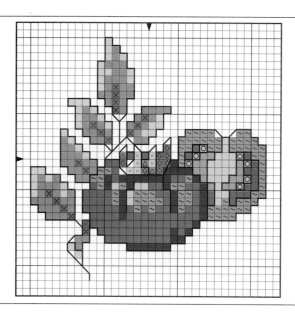

July 24

Design size: 32 wide x 32 high

	Anchor	DMC		Anchor	DMC
▨	46	666	□	842	3013
■	1005	816	△	843	3012
□	6	754	◇	845	730
∿	10/329	351/3340			
▨	323	3825			
○	313	742			
□	259	772			
▨	265	3347			
✕	267	469			

Backstitch:
1005—half tomato
22/814—whole tomato
267—leaves, stems
845—tomato top

July 25

Design size: 28 wide x 40 high

	Anchor	DMC
□	2	blanc
□	259	772
∿	265	3347
✕	267	469
■	268	936
□	95	554
▨	97	553
■	99	552
□	234	762
□	232	453

Backstitch:
268—leaves
99—purple area of turnip
233/452—remaining turnip

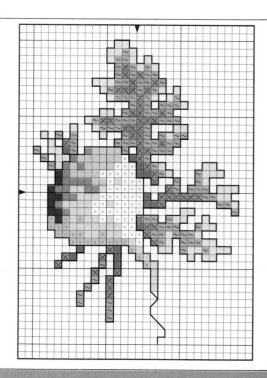

July 26

Design size: 33 wide x 32 high

	Anchor	DMC
▫	2	blanc
▨	9	352
▨	46	666
▫	259	772
△	266	3347
▨	268	469
▨	240	966
✕	243	703
◼	246	986

Backstitch:
1005/816—watermelon meat
268—leaves, stems, top tendril
246—remaining watermelon (except seeds)
879/500—bottom tendril
403/310—seeds

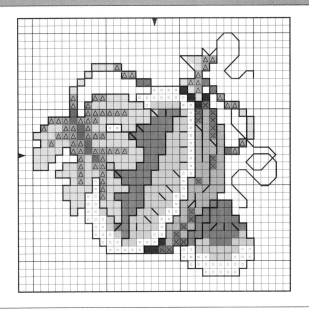

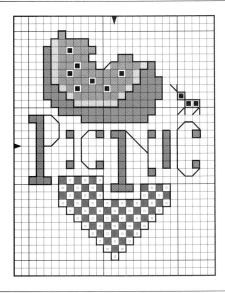

July 27

Design size: 23 wide x 30 high

	Anchor	DMC
▫	2	blanc
▨	1023	3712
▨	334	606
▫	259	772
▨	242	989
▨	161	813
◼	403	310

Backstitch:
1024/3328—watermelon meat
244/702—remaining watermelon
161—lettering
403—ant, napkin

July 28

Design size: 23 wide x 41 high

	Anchor	DMC
▫	2	blanc
∼	24	963
▨	50	605
▨	52	957
▨	46	666
◿	1006	304
▨	45	814
▫	1012	754
∧	311	3827
▨	1002	977
▨	1003/1004	922/920
◎	130	809
▨	131	798
▨	351	400

Backstitch:
52—wings
1006—"RUBY"
45—gem, pink &
  red dress edges
1013/3778—skin
1001/976—ribbon
132/797—vest
351—hair
403/310—eyes

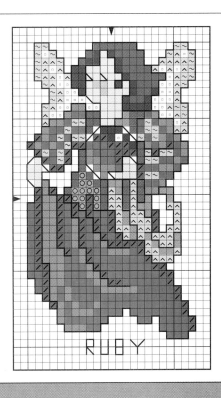

July 29

Design size: 31 wide x 33 high

	Anchor	DMC
▫	2	blanc
▫	301	744
▫	302	743
▫	241	966
▫	1060	3811
▫	130	809
▫	367	738
▫	235	414

French Knots: 400/317
Backstitch:
146/798—lettering
400—remaining outlines

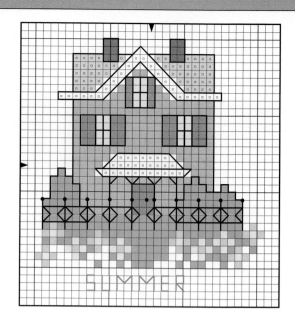

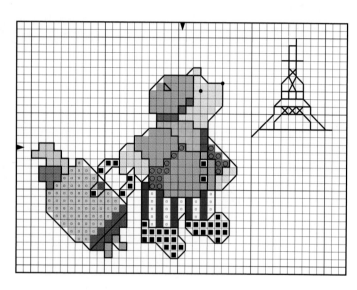

July 30

Design size: 41 wide x 29 high

	Anchor	DMC
▫	2	blanc
⊚	334	606
■	1005	816
	96	3609
	329	3340
	305	743
	241	966
	210	562
	881	945
▫	368	437
	370	434
	234	762
	235	414
■	403	310

French Knots: 403
Backstitch:
1049/3826—bear
403—shoes, buttons,
suitcase handle
400/317—remaining
outlines

July 31

Design size: 40 wide x 31 high

	Anchor	DMC
▫	2	blanc
■	334	606
▫	293	727
△	302	743
	130	809
	146	798
	881	945
	1047	402
	234	762
⊠	399	318
■	403	310

French Knots: 403
Backstitch:
1049/3826—bear (except nose), horn
400/317—helmet, clothes, shoe
403—remaining outlines

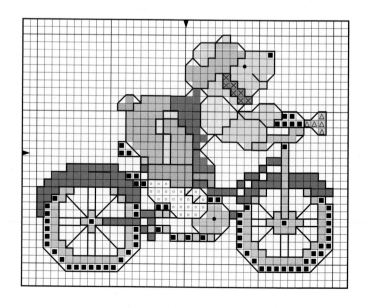

August

August

August 21

August 17

August 2

Gladiolus

August 16

August 9

August 15

August 4

August 22

August 1

August 19

August 5

August 26

berries

August 12

You've got a friend

August 23

August 3

August 11

August 6

August

August 28

August 30

August 10

August 8

August 20

August 27

August 29

August 13

August 18

August 14

August 24

August 31

August 7

August 25

August 1

Design size: 34 wide x 21 high

	Anchor	DMC
	1012	754
	868	353
◎	328	3341
▲	333	608
▫	301	744
	241	966
	885	739
~	891	676
	890	729
	400	317

French Knots: 400
Backstitch:
1007/3772—hair, skin
400—remaining outlines

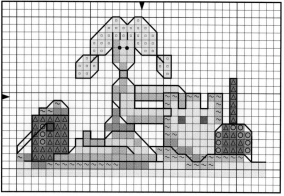

August 3

Design size: 10 wide x 27 high

	Anchor	DMC
	49	3689
♡	50	605
	158	747
▲	167	519
	342	211
✕	108	210
	361	738
◎	362/363	437/436

Backstitch: 400/317

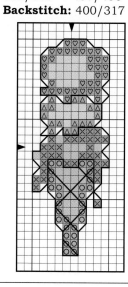

August 2

Design size: 29 wide x 30 high

	Anchor	DMC
	334	606
	1005	816
	45	814
	302	743
	329	3340
	259	772
▫	265	3347
◎	257	905
	246	986

French Knot: 329
Backstitch:
334—"AUGUST"
1005—flowers
46/666—border
329—"Gladiolus"
246—leaves

August 4

Design size: 27 wide x 34 high

	Anchor	DMC		Anchor	DMC
	253	472		349	301
~	265	3347		351	400
▲	262	3363			
	1044	895			
▫	259	772			
◎	266	3347			
✕	268	469			
	347	402			

Backstitch:
1044—avocados
(except pit)
268—leaves
351—stems, branch

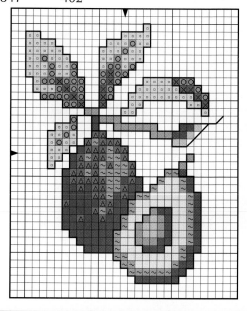

August 5

Design size: 23 wide x 22 high

Anchor	DMC	Backstitch:
2	blanc	370/434—piecrust
387	712	400/317—remaining
334	606	outlines
206	564	
130	809	
109	209	
362	437	
369	435	

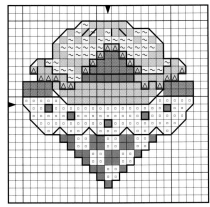

August 6

Design size: 31 wide x 30 high

Anchor	DMC		
2	blanc	**I Backstitch:** 403	
361	738	**Backstitch:**	
1047	402	876—wreath	
1048	3776	98/553—remaining	
875	3813	purple shells	
876	3816	351/400—remaining	
342	211	gold shells	
96	3609	1086—remaining	
231	453	gray shells	
233	452		
1086	839		
403	310		

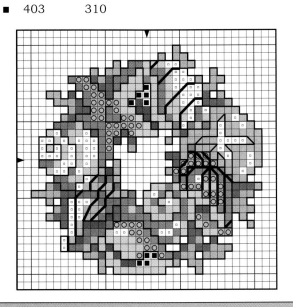

August 7

Design size: 32 wide x 22 high

Anchor	DMC	Backstitch:
2	blanc	262/3363—leaves, stems
386	3823	1033—table, pitcher, stir
292	3078	stick, ice cubes, flower
295	726	petals
264	3348	1002/977—flower centers,
1031	3753	lemons, lemonade line
1033	932	

August 8

Design size: 25 wide x 38 high

Anchor	DMC	Backstitch:
2	blanc	11—sun rays, "AUG," "SUN"s
11	351	160 (2 strands)—line above
302	743	umbrellas
1002	977	1039—zigzag line, "SEA"
160	827	1039 (2 strands)—line under "AUG"
1039	518	162—umbrellas, pail (except
162	517	umbrella handle)
943	422	374 (2 strands)—line under waves
374	420	1050—umbrella handle on pail,
1050	3781	rudders, + signs
French Knots: 1050		1050 (2 strands)—bottom line

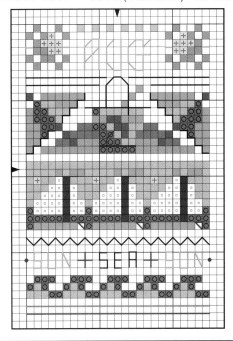

August 9

Design size: 37 wide x 19 high

Anchor	DMC
23	3713
334	606
210	562
129	809
162	517
366	951
347	402
349	301
234	762

French Knot: 403/310
Backstitch:
211/562—outside
   edges of canoe
371/434—paddle,
   remaining canoe
400/317—mouse,
   clothes

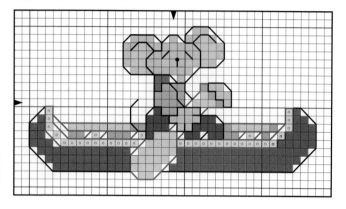

August 10

Design size: 27 wide x 37 high

Anchor	DMC	Anchor	DMC
2	blanc	120	3747
334	606	121	809
1005	816	122	3807
329	3340	231	453
311	3827	233	452
1002	977	403	310
1048	3776		

Backstitch: 403

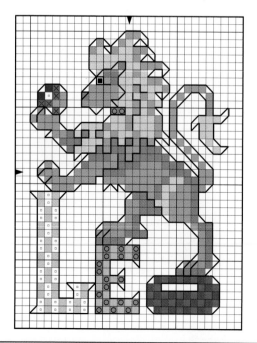

August 11

Design size: 12 wide x 29 high

Anchor	DMC
2	blanc
23	3713
25	3326
334	606
120	3747

Backstitch:
334—straw stripes
235/414—remaining outlines

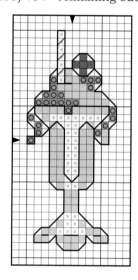

August 12

Design size: 30 wide x 30 high

Anchor	DMC	Anchor	DMC
2	blanc	260	772
386	3823	262	3363
313	742	130	809
329	3340	349	301
361	738	403	310
1002	977		

Backstitch: 400/317

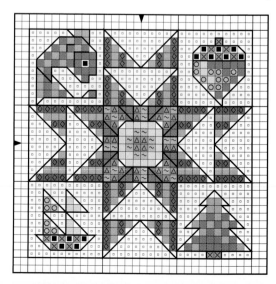

August 13

Design size: 13 wide x 31 high

	Anchor	DMC
▫	2	blanc
■	334	606
■	1005	816
⊠	302	743
□	128	800
▨	129	809
▲	146	798
▨	366	951
～	368	437
■	403	310

Backstitch:
211/562—buttonhole
   threads
370/434—nest
400/317—remaining
   outlines

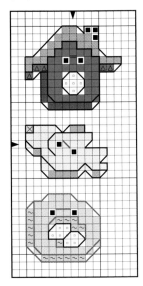

August 15

Design size: 24 wide x 27 high

	Anchor	DMC
▨	8	3824
□	311	3827
□	1043	369
⊙	241	966
□	128	800
▨	129	809
▨	2/231	blanc/453
△	232	452
■	403	310

French Knots: 403
Straight Stitch
(whiskers): 400/317
Backstitch:
403—watermelon
   seeds
400—remaining
   outlines

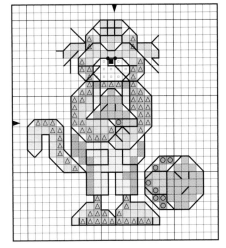

August 14

Design size: 32 wide x 23 high

	Anchor	DMC		Anchor	DMC
▫	2	blanc	□	311	3827
～	1021	761	△	362	437
⊙	895	223	▨	234	762
▨	1024	3328	■	401	413
▨	896	3721			
⊠	891	676			
▨	875	3813			
□	128	800			

French Knots: 401
Backstitch:
905/3021—border
401—remaining outlines

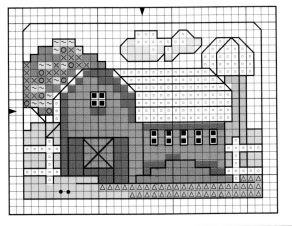

August 16

Design size: 30 wide x 25 high

	Anchor	DMC
▨	842	3013
▨	843	3012
▨	928	3811
▨	311	3827
▨	1002	977
⊙	1048	3776
▨	1004	920
▨	357	433
▨	231	453
■	403	310

Backstitch:
1004—basket weave
   lines
403—remaining
   basket, fish

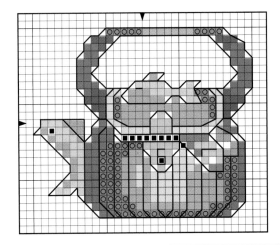

August 17

Design size: 23 wide x 30 high

Anchor	DMC		Anchor	DMC
2	blanc		1048	3776
1012	754		376	3774
868	353		388	3033
301	744		400	317
302	743			
214	368			
158	747			
167	519			
128	800			
130	809			
1047	402			

French Knots:
379/840—sunflower
400—eyes
Backstitch:
217/561—leaf, stem
379—sunflower
400—remaining outlines

August 18

Design size: 39 wide x 19 high

Anchor	DMC
6	754
159	3325
162	517

French Knots: 162
Backstitch:
162—lettering, birds (except beaks & legs)
349/301—beaks, legs

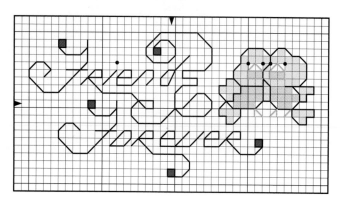

August 19

Design size: 18 wide x 15 high

Anchor	DMC
2	blanc
9	352
11	351
301	744
215	320

Backstitch: 400/317

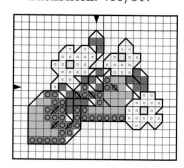

August 20

Design size: 21 wide x 45 high

Anchor	DMC
2	blanc
23	3713
334	606
162	517
880	3774
368	437
234	762
399	318

French Knot: 403/310
Backstitch:
334—shirt anchor
162—blue anchor
370/434—rope
400/317—remaining outlines

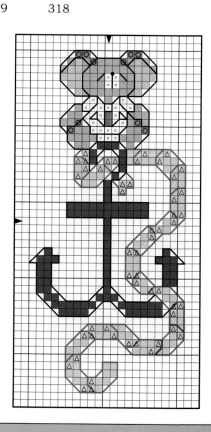

August 21

Design size: 35 wide x 25 high

Anchor	DMC
2	blanc
334	606
305	743
146	798
881	945
1047	402
234	762
399	318
403	310

French Knots: 403

Backstitch:

146—lounge chair
1049/3826—bear
400/317—towel, cat, swimsuit
403—sunglasses

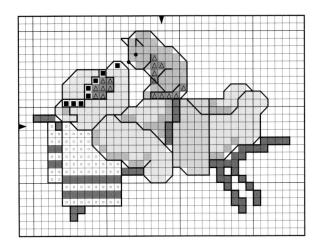

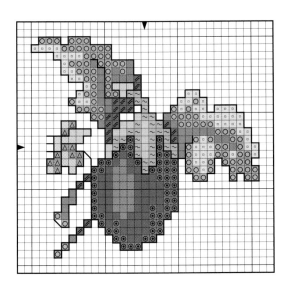

August 22

Design size: 31 wide x 29 high

Anchor	DMC
87	3607
94	917
302	743
259	772
265	3347
267	469
268	937
842	3013
843	3012
342	211
97	554
102	550

Backstitch:

302 (2 strands)—flower center
268—stems, plant leaves
845/730—eggplant leaves
102—flower, eggplant

August 23

Design size: 26 wide x 38 high

Anchor	DMC
2	blanc
1012	754
313	742
329	3340
300	745
240	966
210	562
95	554
349	301

French Knot: 403/310

Backstitch:

210—leaves, stem, lettering
98/553—purple flower, dress
349—remaining outlines

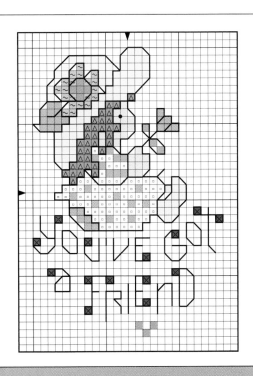

August 24

Design size: 15 wide x 35 high

	Anchor	DMC
▫	2	blanc
■	334	606
■	323	3825
■	305	743
■	240	966
■	160	827
✖	170	3765
■	96	3609

Backstitch:
334—underlines
170—"NOAH"
400/317—ark

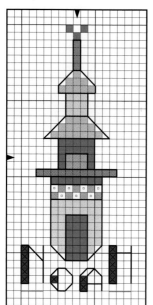

August 25

Design size: 14 wide x 46 high

	Anchor	DMC
▫	2	blanc
■	314	741
■	305	743
■	253	472
■	257	905
☐	128	800
◹	129	809
∽	368	437
■	403	310

French Knot: 403
❙ **Backstitch** (2 strands): 403
Backstitch:
258/904—leaves
349/301—flame, wick,
  nest, sunflower
400/317—remaining
  outlines

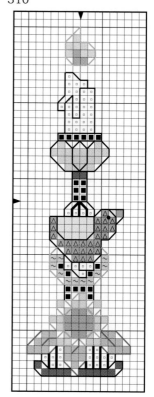

August 26

Design size: 65 wide x 23 high

	Anchor	DMC		Anchor	DMC
▫	2	blanc	■	302	743
☐	1020	3713	■	259	772
■	895	223	■	265	3347
■	1006	304	☐	128	800

French Knot: 1005/816
Backstitch:
1005—berries, lettering
302—flower centers
257/905—leaves, stems, vines

1034/931—flower
  petals

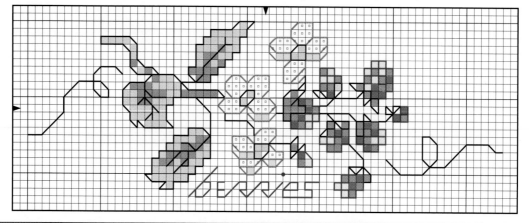

August 27

Design size: 38 wide x 42 high

	Anchor	DMC
▫	2	blanc
■	334	606
☐	128	800
■	129	809
■	146	798
■	1002	977
☐	276	739
■	376	3774
■	1084	840
☐	234	762
■	399	318
■	403	310

Backstitch:
1086/839—tabby cat
400/317—remaining outlines

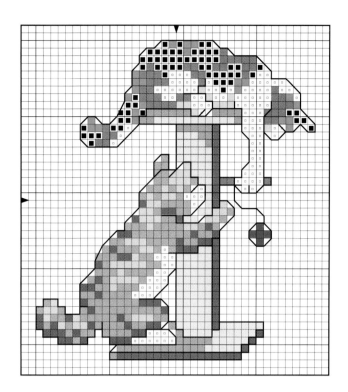

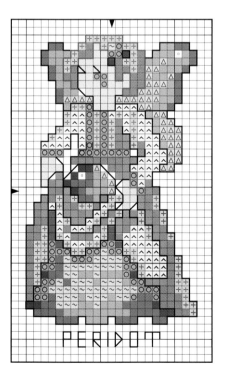

August 28

Design size: 23 wide x 41 high

	Anchor	DMC
▫	2	blanc
∼	48	3689
◎	50	605
■	54	956
☐	1012	754
∧	300	745
✛	311	3827
■	1002	977
■	1001	976
△	259	772
■	254	3348
■	255	907
■	245	986

Backstitch:
54—hair flower, pink dress trim
255—wings
245—hair leaves, green dress edges,
    gem, "PERIDOT"
1001—skin, remaining dress
370/434—hair
403/310—eyes

August 29

Design size: 34 wide x 38 high

Anchor	DMC
2	blanc
334	606
386	3823
891	676
225	702
2/234	blanc/762
399	318
403	310

French Knots: 228/700
Backstitch:
334 (2 strands)—fly
228—fishing line, lettering
400/317—reel
403—hook

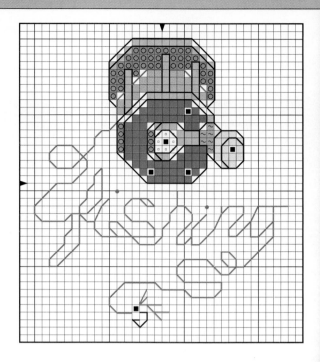

August 30

Design size: 42 wide x 27 high

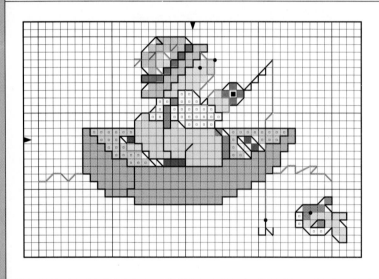

Anchor	DMC
2	blanc
390	3033
334	606
311	3827
203	564
211	562
128	800
130	809
881	945
403	310

French Knots: 403
Backstitch:
334—hat flies, shirt
plaid, fishing line
211—hat fly
146/798—water
1049/3826—bear
400/317—hat, remaining
shirt, pants, reel, pole,
boat, fish
403—hat fly, fishing line
hook

August 31

Design size: 37 wide x 34 high

Anchor	DMC
2	blanc
73	963
334	606
129	809
146	798
367	738
234	762
403	310

French Knots: 403
Backstitch:
334—"C"
146—hat, shirt, & pant stripes
370/434—bat
400/317—cat (except face),
remaining clothes, shoes
403—face

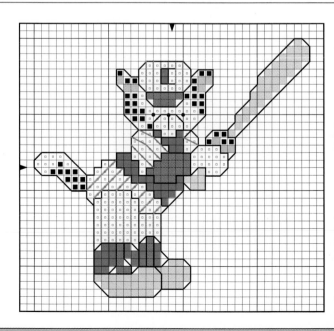

September 28

September 17

September 2

September 16

September 9

September 18

SAPPHIRE

September 20

September 7

September 25

September 5

September 26

September 29

September 14

September 27

September 30

September 8

September 4

September 11

September 19

September 10

September 1

September 21

September 22

September 23

September 15

September 12

September 3

September 24

September 13

September 6

September 1

Design size: 29 wide x 22 high

Anchor	DMC
2	blanc
334	606
303	742
293	727
942	738
260	772
367	437
376	3774
379	840
2/234	blanc/762
399	318

French Knots: 403/310
Backstitch:
268/469—vest, grass
371/434—bear, shoes,
   branch, logs, fire
400/317—remaining
   outlines

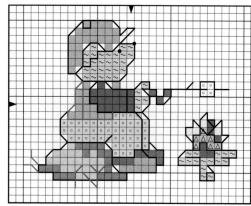

September 2

Design size: 30 wide x 30 high

Anchor	DMC
386	3823
301	744
1002	977
206	564
208	563
211	562
103/85	211/3609
86	3608
98	553
101	550

Backstitch:
1001/976—flower
   center
211—leaves, stems
86—"Aster"
99/552—flowers,
   "SEPTEMBER"
101—border

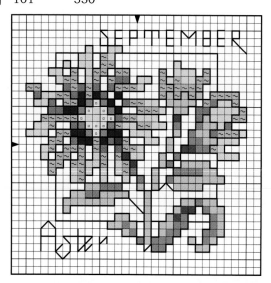

September 3

Design size: 35 wide x 17 high

Anchor	DMC
2	blanc
334	606
391	3033
392	642
393	640
399	318
236	3799
403	310

French Knots: 403
Backstitch:
1005/816—apple (except stem)
393—remaining outlines

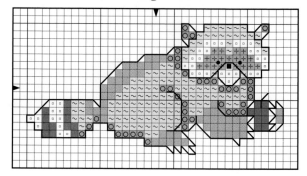

September 4

Design size: 24 wide x 30 high

Anchor	DMC
275	746
10	351
13	347
20	815
361	738
362	437
365	435
265	3347
267	469
358	801
1041	844

Backstitch: 1041

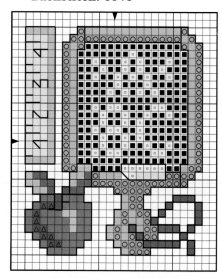

September 5

Design size: 21 wide x 27 high

Anchor	DMC	Backstitch:
2	blanc	38/961—muzzle
926	712	1049/3826—cat (except
1038	519	muzzle & eyes)
885	739	392—cap bill stripes
1047	402	400/317—remaining cap
1048	3776	403—eyes
830	644	
392	642	
403	310	

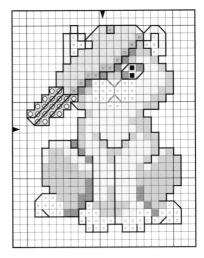

September 6

Design size: 30 wide x 30 high

Anchor	DMC	Backstitch:
2	blanc	2—white flowers
332	946	1006/304—apples
46	666	(except stems)
1005	816	269/936—leaves
311	3827	403/310—stems
259	772	
265	3347	
268	469	

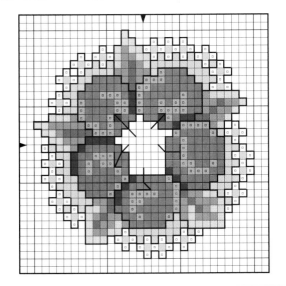

September 7

Design size: 23 wide x 18 high

Anchor	DMC
2	blanc
334	606
1012	754
241	966
403	310

French Knots: 403

Backstitch:
1024/3328—mouth
1013/3778—skin
403—hair
400/317—remaining outlines

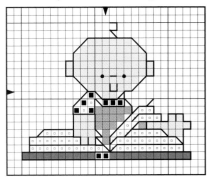

September 8

Design size: 25 wide x 38 high

Anchor	DMC	French Knots: 403
2	blanc	**Backstitch:**
895	223	896—"SCHOOL,"
896	3721	"SCHOOL"
891	676	1045—dashes in
1045	436	alphabet
209	913	273—alphabet lines,
211	562	pencils
273	645	403—remaining
403	310	lettering

September 9

Design size: 26 wide x 21 high

	Anchor	DMC		Anchor	DMC
▫	2	blanc	☐	2/9159	blanc/828
■	9046	321	■	1038	519
☐	328	3341	■	122	3807
◉	333	608			
☐	301	744			
☐	302	743			
☐	241	966			

Backstitch:
122—backpack
400/317—remaining outlines

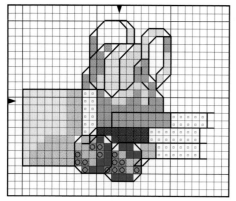

September 10

Design size: 27 wide x 31 high

	Anchor	DMC		Anchor	DMC
▫	2	blanc	■	1048	3776
◉	48	3689	■	265	3347
■	50	605	☐	1092	995
▲	57	602	☐	186	959
☐	1012	754	☐	342	211
~	868	353	■	109	209
☐	311	3827			
■	1002	977			

Backstitch: 403/310

September 11

Design size: 16 wide x 29 high

	Anchor	DMC		Anchor	DMC
▫	2	blanc	☐	9159	828
☐	1012	754	■	1039	518
▫	868	353	■	378	841
△	328	3341	■	403	310
■	333	608			
☐	300	745			
☐	311	3827			

French Knots: 400/317
Backstitch: 400

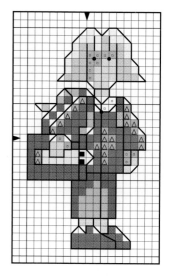

September 12

Design size: 30 wide x 30 high

	Anchor	DMC		Anchor	DMC
▫	2	blanc	▲	131	798
☐	386	3823	☐	96	3609
~	1092	995	■	98	553
☐	186	959	■	100	327
◉	188	3812	☐	361	738
☐	128	800			
■	130	809			

Backstitch: 400/317

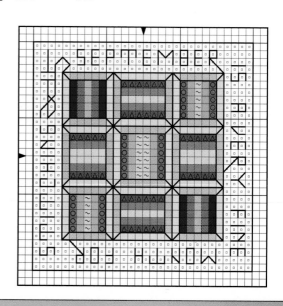

112

September 13

Design size: 31 wide x 17 high

	Anchor	DMC
	2	blanc
	9	352
	11	351
	311	3827
	314	741
	206	564
	928	3811
	129	809
	2/231	blanc/453

French Knots: 403/310
Backstitch:
978/312—blue book, clothes
400/317—remaining outlines

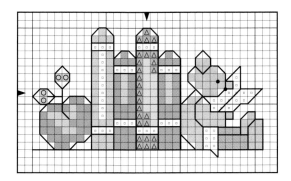

September 15

Design size: 23 wide x 26 high

	Anchor	DMC
	1020	3713
	894	223
	1027	3722
	1043	369

Backstitch:
1027—lettering, flower
210/562—remaining outlines

September 14

Design size: 28 wide x 26 high

	Anchor	DMC
	2	blanc
	10	351
	301	744
	1043	369
	241	966
	1092	995
	185	964
	128	800
	234	762
	235	414

French Knots:
400/317
Backstitch:
11/3705—lighthouse
   stripes
244/702—frame
130/809—clouds
400—remaining
   outlines

September 16

Design size: 31 wide x 28 high

	Anchor	DMC
	46	666
	240	966
	243	703
	246	986
	1003	922
	311	3827
	1001	976
	1004	920
	403	310

Backstitch: 403

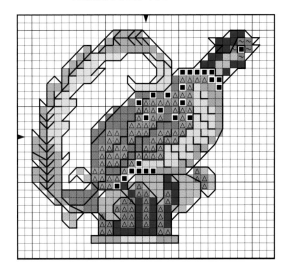

September 17

Design size: 21 wide x 28 high

Anchor	DMC
8	3824
11	351
295	726
1043	369
241	966
376	3774
399	318

French Knot: 403/310
Backstitch: 401/413

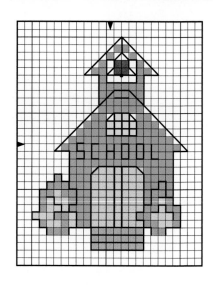

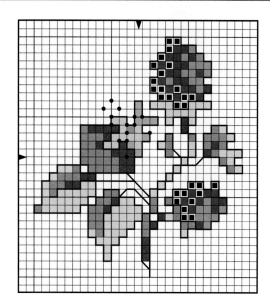

September 18

Design size: 27 wide x 30 high

Anchor	DMC
63	3804
65	3685
259	772
266	3347
268	469
347	402
349	301
403	310

French Knots: 403
Backstitch:
268—leaves, stems
351/400—flower
403—berries

September 19

Design size: 15 wide x 33 high

Anchor	DMC
2	blanc
24	963
300	745
311	3827
167	519
136	799
234	762
399	318
401	413

French Knots: 403/310
Straight Stitch (whiskers): 403
Backstitch: 400/317

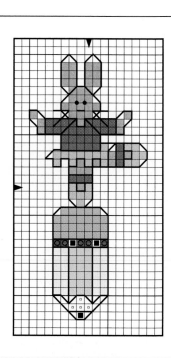

September 20

Design size: 26 wide x 26 high

	Anchor	DMC			Anchor	DMC
▫	2	blanc		▫	129	809
▪	108	210		⊙	369	435
▫	1012	754		▫	390/391	3033/3782
▪	336	758		~	392	642
▪	328	3341		▪	401	413
▫	300	745		**French Knot:** 400/317		
▫	311	3827		**Backstitch:** 400		
▫	185	964				

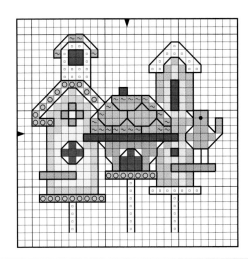

September 21

Design size: 15 wide x 41 high

	Anchor	DMC
▪	334	606
~	8	3824
▫	868	353
▫	302	743
▫	254	3348
▪	1072	992
▫	129	809
▪	146	798
■	403	310

French Knot: 403
Backstitch:
370/434—pencil, apple stem
401/413—remaining outlines

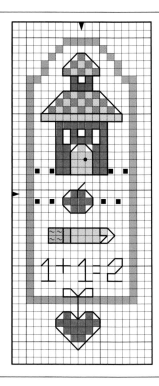

September 22

Design size: 13 wide x 37 high

	Anchor	DMC
▫	2	blanc
▪	334	606
▪	1005	816
▫	8	3824
▫	305	743
~	306	783
▫	241	966
▫	875	3813
▫	276	739
■	403	310

Backstitch:
2 (2 strands)—"A+"
334 (2 strands)—thread on slate & pencil buttons
245/986 (2 strands)—thread on apple button
370/434—apple stem, wood pencil lines
400/317—remaining outlines

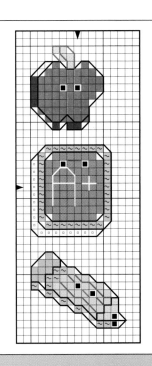

September 23

Design size: 18 wide x 48 high

	Anchor	DMC
	85	3609
	300	745
	311	3827
	261	989
	159	3325
	167	519
	117	341

Backstitch: 400/317

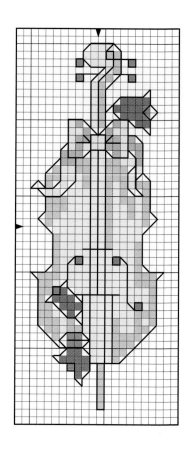

September 24

Design size: 35 wide x 41 high

	Anchor	DMC
	387	712
	334	606
	96	3609
	242	989
	361	738
	1001	976
	370	434
	403	310

Backstitch:
1005/816—apple
211/562—leaf
371/433—apple stem, strap,
   dog (except eye & nose)
400/317—books
403—eye, nose

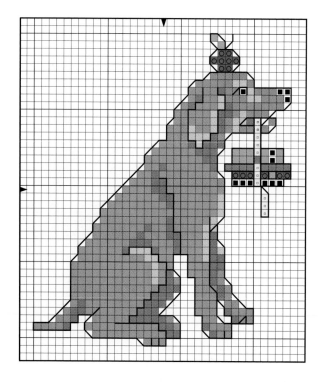

September 25

Design size: 33 wide x 35 high

	Anchor	DMC
□	2	blanc
∼	885	739
▨	778/868	3774/353
▨	337	3776
◉	313	742
▨	307	783
▨	261	989
▨	129	809
△	1013	3778
∧	1008	3773
▫	933	543
▪	376/378	3774/841
∞	366	951
⊠	347	402

French Knots: 400/317
Backstitch:
246/986—leaves, stems
347—straw in hat,
   hair, arms
349/301—face, flowers,
   legs
400—remaining
   outlines

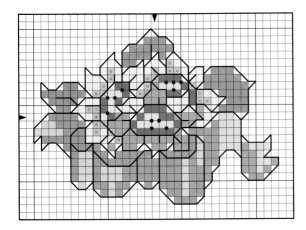

September 26

Design size: 33 wide x 23 high

	Anchor	DMC
▫	313	742
□	301	744
▨	891	676
▨	261	989
▨	2/342	blanc/211
▨	108	210
□	347	402
▨	1084	840

French Knots: 400/317
Backstitch: 400

September 27

Design size: 34 wide x 32 high

	Anchor	DMC
□	2	blanc
□	259	772
▨	266	3347
▨	268	469
▨	120	3747
▨	109	209
◉	111	553
▨	347	402
▨	349	301
▨	351	400

Backstitch:
268—leaves, leaf stem
111—grapes
351—branch, grape stems

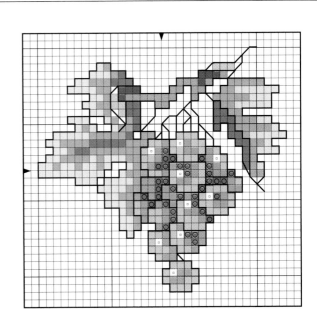

September 28

Design size: 23 wide x 41 high

	Anchor	DMC
□	2	blanc
♡	50	605
□	1012	754
+	868	353
~	300	745
∞	311/1002	3827/977
□	128	800
△	130	809
✕	131	798
■	132	797
□	342	211
⊙	109	209
■	111	553
╱	347	402
■	349	301

Eyelet (end of wand): 102/550
Backstitch:
1013/3778—skin
130—wings
132—headband, gem, blue
   edges of dress, "SAPPHIRE"
111—ribbon
349—remaining wand &
   dress, hair
403/310—eyes

September 29

Design size: 46 wide x 21 high

	Anchor	DMC
□	1043	369
■	241	966
■	210	562
□	342	211
■	96	3609
■	110	208

Backstitch:
211/562—leaves, stems
110—grapes

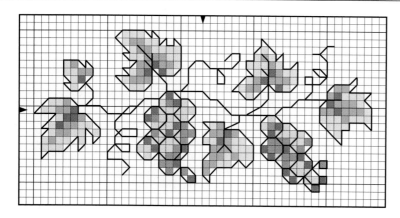

September 30

Design size: 35 wide x 37 high

	Anchor	DMC
□	2	blanc
■	334	606
◉	1005	816
□	302	743
□	928	3811
■	168	3810
□	933	543
■	378	841
■	936	632
▫	234	762
■	403	310

French Knots: 403
Backstitch:
209/913—pant stripes
169/806—fish (except eye)
936—cat
400/317—clothes
403—fish eye, pan

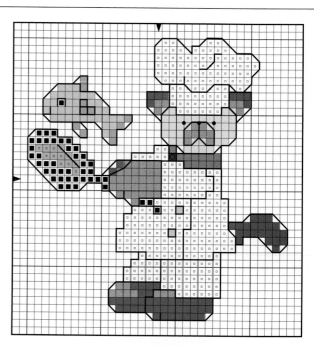

October

October 24

October 17

October 28

October 10

October 12

October 18

October 26

October 30

October 1

October 27

October 7

October 9

October 19

October 20

October 22

October 13

October 23

October

October 2

October 16

October 5

October 8

October 3

October 11

October 25

October 14

October 21

October 31

October 15

October 4

October 29

October 6

October 1

Design size: 23 wide x 21 high

	Anchor	DMC
□	2	blanc
∞	336	758
▨	338	922
~	311	3827
▨	362	437
▨	347	402
✕	349	301

French Knot: 400/317
Backstitch: 400

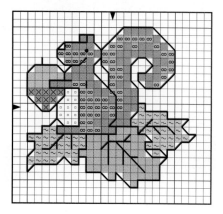

October 2

Design size: 29 wide x 29 high

	Anchor	DMC	Backstitch:
□	885	739	324—"Calendula"
▨	303	742	326—flower (except
~	324	721	center), "OCTOBER"
▨	326/1004	720/920	246—leaves, stem
□	301	744	358/801—flower center,
⊙	363	436	border
△	365	435	
▨	259	772	
▨	265	3347	
✕	257	905	
▨	246	986	

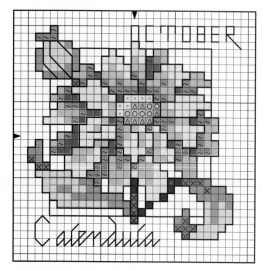

October 3

Design size: 25 wide x 26 high

	Anchor	DMC
□	2	blanc
▨	314	741
▨	128	800
▨	881	945
■	403	310

Backstitch:
1049/3826—bear, pumpkin (except face)
400/317—costume, handle
403—face

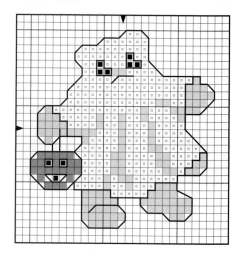

October 4

Design size: 27 wide x 24 high

	Anchor	DMC	Backstitch:
□	2	blanc	879/500—leaves
■	1003	922	130/809—flower
∧	300	745	351—branch, stems,
▨	302	743	pear (except bottom)
▨	259	772	403/310—pear bottom
+	875	3813	
▨	876	3816	
□	128	800	
~	347	402	
⊙	349	301	
■	351	400	

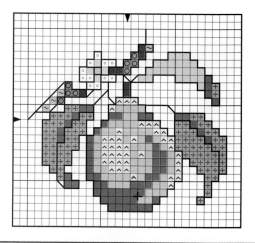

October 5

Design size: 26 wide x 30 high

Anchor	DMC	Anchor	DMC
2	blanc	168	3810
894	223	129	809
46	666	136	799
1012	754	899	3782
868	353		
1003	922		
300	745		
311	3827		
875	3813		
928	3811		

French Knots: 400/317
Backstitch:
47/321—jacket stripes
903/640—hair, skin, leaves, wind lines, shoes
400—remaining outlines

October 6

Design size: 32 wide x 31 high

Anchor	DMC	Anchor	DMC
2	blanc	146	798
314	741	349	301
332	946	403	310
301	744		
265	3347		
120	3747		
130	809		

Backstitch:
268/469—wreath
403—remaining outlines

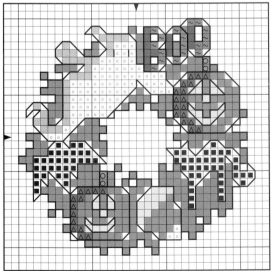

October 7

Design size: 25 wide x 20 high

Anchor	DMC
2	blanc
73	963
75	962
76	961
1012	754
128	800
347	402

French Knots: 146/798
Backstitch:
76—dress, headband
1024/3328—mouth
1013/3778—skin (except nose)
306/783—halo, wand
349/301—hair, nose
146—wings

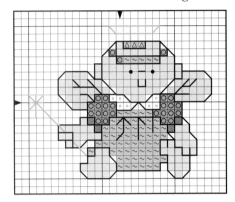

October 8

Design size: 25 wide x 38 high

Anchor	DMC
2	blanc
324	721
326	720
302	743
205	912
211	562
108	210
110	208
403	310

French Knot: 211
Eyelet (spiders): 403
Backstitch:
326—lettering
211—stems
403—webs

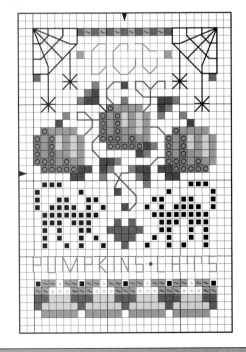

October 9

Design size: 31 wide x 17 high

	Anchor	DMC
▫	2	blanc
■	334	606
▫	1012	754
⊙	300	745
▫	206	564
▫	128	800
✕	130	809
～	347	402
■	403	310

French Knots: 349/301
Backstitch:
1024/3328—mouth
334—string
1013/3778—skin (except
  nose)
349—nose, hair
400/317—remaining
  outlines

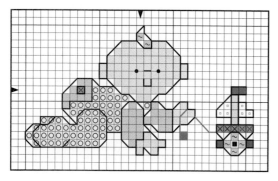

October 10

Design size: 30 wide x 32 high

	Anchor	DMC
▫	2	blanc
⊙	50	605
■	54	956
■	1005	816
▫	300	745
▫	302	743
▫	314	741
▫	1092	995
△	186	959
■	188	3812
✕	1004	920

Backstitch: 403/310

October 11

Design size: 27 wide x 22 high

	Anchor	DMC
▣	25	3326
▫	292	3078
▫	311	3827
～	1039	518
■	162	517

Backstitch:
162—lettering
369/435—bow

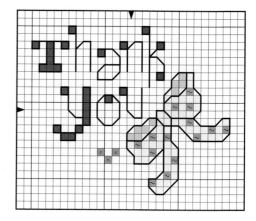

October 12

Design size: 30 wide x 30 high

	Anchor	DMC
▫	2	blanc
▫	313	742
▫	316	970
▫	265	3347
■	403	310

Backstitch: 400/317

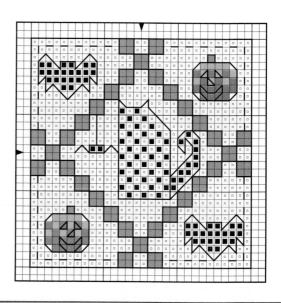

October 13

Design size: 36 wide x 20 high

	Anchor	DMC
■	1023	3712
◎	323	3825
■	264	3348
△	875	3813
□	347	402
~	349	301

Backstitch: 357/433

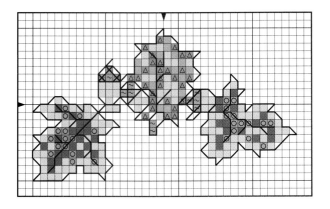

October 14

Design size: 24 wide x 24 high

	Anchor	DMC
□	881	945
~	336	758
◎	313	742
□	301	744
□	1043	369
■	241	966
■	378	841

Backstitch:
210/562—vine
379/840—stitching lines
401/413—remaining outlines

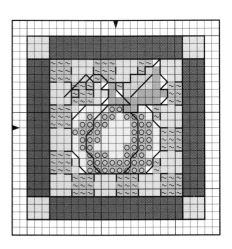

October 15

Design size: 26 wide x 26 high

	Anchor	DMC		Anchor	DMC
▫	2	blanc	~	347	402
■	46	666	◎	349	301
■	1005	816	✕	351	400
■	329	3340		**Backstitch:**	
∿	332	946		1005—apple	
■	240	966		246—leaves	
△	243	703		352/300—branch,	
■	246	986		stems	

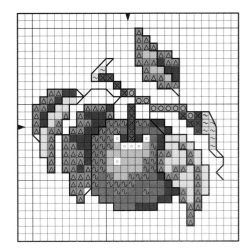

October 16

Design size: 34 wide x 23 high

	Anchor	DMC
□	313	742
■	330	947
◎	333/1004	608/920
■	341	918
□	842	3013
△	843	3012
■	845	730

Backstitch:
341—pumpkin
845—stem, vine, leaves

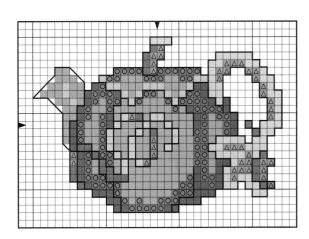

October 17

Design size: 34 wide x 27 high

Anchor	DMC
275	746
314	741
330	947
333/1004	608/920
341	918
301	744
302	743
842	3013
843	3012
845	730

Backstitch:
341—pumpkin
845—leaves, stem, tendrils
1004—blossom

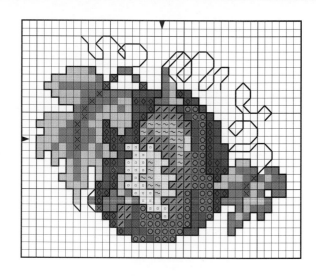

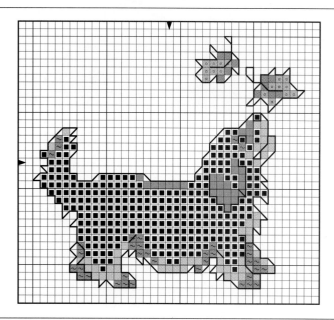

October 18

Design size: 37 wide x 33 high

Anchor	DMC
313	742
329	3340
347	402
349	301
399	318
403	310

Backstitch:
370/434—leaves
403—dog

October 19

Design size: 64 wide x 19 high

Anchor	DMC
2	blanc
313	742
323	3825
1043	369
241	966
369	435

Anchor	DMC
234	762
403	310

Backstitch:
210/562—leaves, stem, tendrils
371/434—pumpkin
400/317—cat (except eye & nose)
403—eye, nose

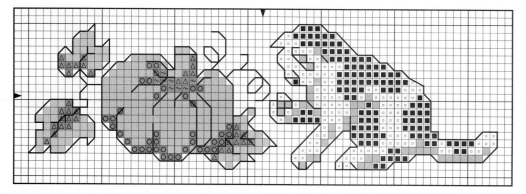

October 20

Design size: 29 wide x 23 high

	Anchor	DMC			Anchor	DMC
▫	2	blanc		♥	109	209
☐	386	3823		△	349	301
▨	1022	760		☐	234	762
▨	85	3609		◎	399	318
~	8	3824		■	400	317
✕	314	741		**French Knot:** 401/413		
☐	302	743		**Backstitch:** 401		
▨	875	3813				

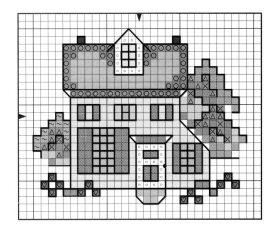

October 21

Design size: 23 wide x 36 high

	Anchor	DMC
✕	334	606
∿	313	742
☐	292	3078
~	295	726
▫	305	743
☐	1043	369
△	241	966
▨	210	562
▨	1047	402
■	403	310

Backstitch:

334—lettering
210—leaves, green checks
1048/3776—petals
1049/3826—flower center, sun

October 22

Design size: 58 wide x 18 high

	Anchor	DMC			Anchor	DMC
▫	2	blanc		▨	894	223
☐	1020	3713		◎	1027	3722
				Backstitch: 1027		

October 23

Design size: 16 wide x 37 high

	Anchor	DMC
□	2	blanc
▨	313	742
▨	316	970
~	305	743
▨	241	966
▨	128	800
■	403	310

Backstitch:
334/606 (2 strands)—thread
210/562 (2 strands)—thread
210—stem
370/434—remaining pumpkin, candy corn
400/317—ghost

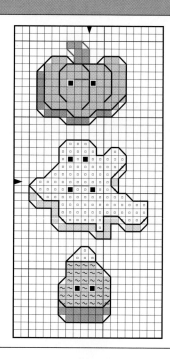

October 24

Design size: 30 wide x 30 high

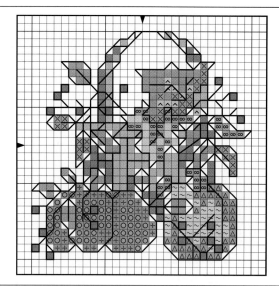

	Anchor	DMC
⊠	338	922
▨	13	347
◉	323	3825
⊞	330	947
~	302	743
◺	314	741
	853/852	372/3047
▨	854	371
▨	214	368
⌃	336	758
□	347	402
⊗	349	301

Backstitch:
211/562—green
   leaves, berry stems
400/317—remaining
   outlines

October 25

Design size: 28 wide x 39 high

	Anchor	DMC
□	2	blanc
▨	1021	761
▨	1022	760
□	300	745
~	311	3827
▨	253	472
◺	858	524
▨	120	3747
▨	158	747
▨	368	437
▨	378	841

French Knot: 400/317
Backstitch:
379/840—lettering
400—remaining outlines

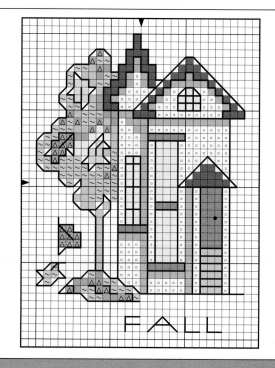

October 26

Design size: 29 wide x 27 high

	Anchor	DMC
	2	blanc
■	334	606
□	120	3747
~	145	809
▨	146	798
□	1047	402
▨	1048	3776
⊠	349	301
■	403	310

French Knots: 403
Backstitch:
145—water
400/317—remaining outlines

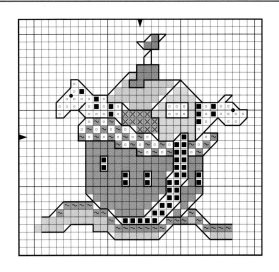

October 27

Design size: 20 wide x 53 high

	Anchor	DMC
□	2	blanc
▨	24	963
▨	334	606
▨	162	517
□	367	738
▨	234	762

French Knots: 403/310
Backstitch:
1005/816—inner border
162—outer border
400/317—remaining outlines

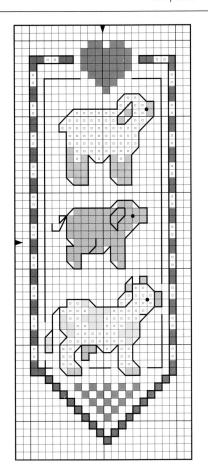

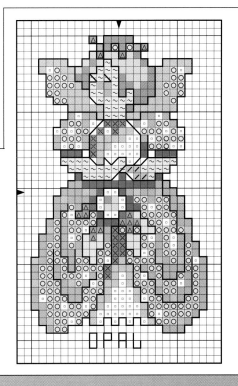

October 28

Design size: 24 wide x 41 high

	Anchor	DMC		Anchor	DMC
□	2	blanc	□	259	772
⊙	48	3689	▲	265	3347
▨	50	605	▨	267	469
▨	54	956	□	120	3747
~	1012	754	⊠	121	809
▨	868	353			
□	311	3827			
▨	1002	977			

Backstitch:
54—pink edges of
   dress, hair flowers

1013/3778—skin
1001/976—hair,
   dress flower
267—leaves
120—wings
121—"OPAL"
122/3807—gem,
   remaining dress
403/310—eyes

October 29

Design size: 27 wide x 32 high

	Anchor	DMC
□	2	blanc
■	334	606
□	311	3827
■	399	318
■	403	310

Backstitch:
1005/816—"PHONE," "PHONE"
146/798—"sweet"
403—phone

October 30

Design size: 41 wide x 30 high

	Anchor	DMC
□	2	blanc
■	334	606
△	328	3341
□	295	726
□	253	472
■	257	905
□	9159	828
■	1039	518
+	387	712
□	881	945
~	1047	402
■	1048	3776
□	2/234	blanc/762
■	234	762
⊚	399	318
■	403	310

French Knots: 403
Backstitch:
162/517—lettering
1049/3826—bear
   (except nose)
403—nose, antennae
400/317—remaining
   outlines

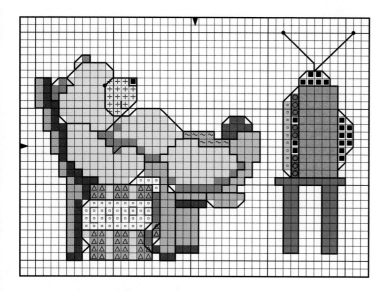

October 31

Design size: 26 wide x 32 high

	Anchor	DMC
□	2	blanc
□	323	3825
⊠	330	947
■	234	762
■	403	310

French Knot: 330
Backstitch:
330—lettering
235/414—ghost (except face)
403—face, string, spider

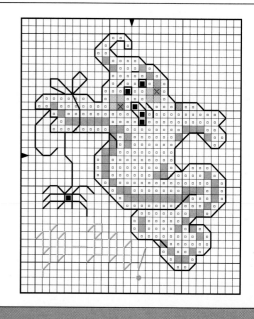

November

NOVEMBER
Chrysanthemum

November

November 23

November 24

November 15

November 2

November 26

November 22

November 16

November 18

November 9

November 27

November 11

November 29

November 25

November 17

November 6

132

November 8

November 28

November 10

November 19

November 13

November 4

November 21

November 30

November 5

November 7

November 20

November 14

November 12

November 3

November 1

November 1

Design size: 31 wide x 23 high

	Anchor	DMC
▫	2	blanc
◼	334	606
◼	96	3609
☐	301	744
⊠	302	743
◻	1032	3752
☐	881	945
◻	1047	402
◎	1049	3826
◼	403	310

French Knot: 403
Backstitch:
1048/3776—flame
1049—bear (except eyes & nose)
400/317—clothes, pillow, candle
403—eyes, nose, candleholder

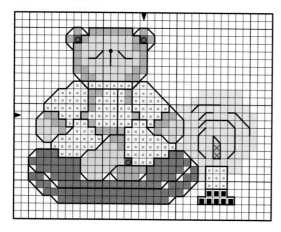

November 3

Design size: 31 wide x 23 high

	Anchor	DMC		Anchor	DMC
▫	2	blanc	≈	349	301
☐	293	727	◼	351	400
◻	305	743			
△	306	783			
⊠	1003	922			
◻	240	966			
◎	243	703			
◼	246	986			
◻	347	402			

Backstitch:
1003—lemon
246—leaves, stems
351—branch

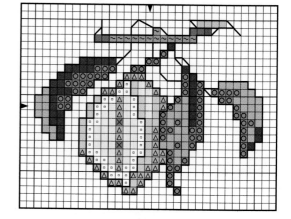

November 2

Design size: 29 wide x 30 high

	Anchor	DMC
▫	2	blanc
☐	313	742
▣	1003	922
◼	326/1004	720/920
☐	301	744
◼	206	564
△	208	563
◼	211	562
◼	371	434

Backstitch:
1003—"Chrysanthemum"
326—flower, "NOVEMBER"
211—leaves
371—border

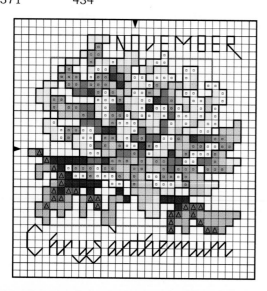

November 4

Design size: 28 wide x 24 high

	Anchor	DMC
◼	334	606
◼	47	321
▫	313	742
△	329	3340
☐	301	744
◻	1042	504
◻	875	3813
◻	342	211
◼	109	209
☐	367	738

Backstitch:
217/561—leaves, tendril
370/434—basket
400/317—remaining outlines

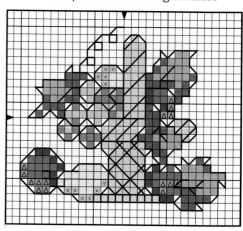

November 5

Design size: 23 wide x 20 high

	Anchor	DMC
▫	2	blanc
■	334	606
☐	1012	754
☐	342	211
△	109	209
◎	347	402
▨	370	434
▨	398	415
■	236	3799

French Knots: 370
Backstitch:
1024/3328—mouth
1005/816—turkey's
   comb
1013/3778—skin
370—hair, turkey legs
236—remaining outlines

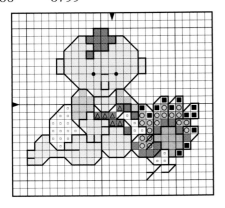

November 7

Design size: 26 wide x 21 high

	Anchor	DMC
☐	367	738
△	369	435
▨	234	762
◎	399	318

French Knots: 401/413
Backstitch:
371/434—brown cat (except nose)
400/317—remaining outlines

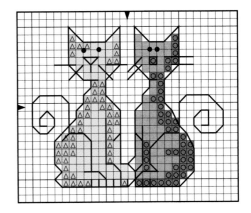

November 6

Design size: 31 wide x 31 high

	Anchor	DMC
▫	2	blanc
☐	361	738
▨	260	772
▨	262	3363
≈	1047	402
▨	1048	3776
▨	232	453
■	403	310

Backstitch: 403

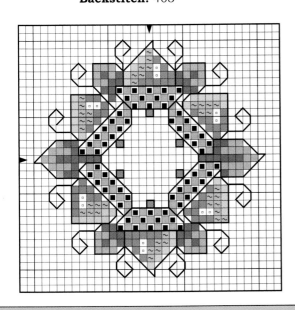

November 8

Design size: 25 wide x 38 high

	Anchor	DMC
▨	891	676
▨	1001/1002	976/977
▨	355	975
◙	265	3347
▨	268	469
▨	109	209
▨	111	553

French Knots: 268
Backstitch:
355 (2 strands)—
   bottom line
268—vines
111—lettering,
   zigzag line

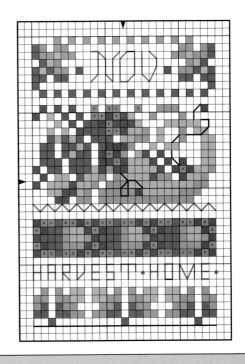

November 9

Design size: 24 wide x 22 high

	Anchor	DMC
	313	742
	324	721
	301	744
	240	966
	216	502
	9159	828
	1038/1039	519/518

French Knots: 400/317
Backstitch:
210/562—leaves, stems
400—remaining outlines

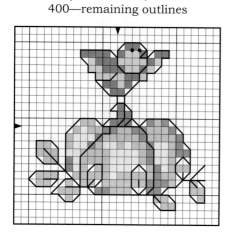

November 11

Design size: 29 wide x 26 high

	Anchor	DMC
	2	blanc
	334	606
	293	727
	241	966
	161	813
	342	211
	881	945
	378	841
	403	310

French Knots: 403
Backstitch:
1049/3826—bear
400/317—hat,
  clothes, skis
403—poles, boots

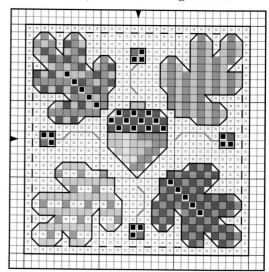

November 10

Design size: 33 wide x 27 high

	Anchor	DMC
	2	blanc
	120	3747
	121	809
	146	798
	2/231	blanc/453
	232	452
	233	451
	403	310

Backstitch:
349/301—border
403—remaining outlines

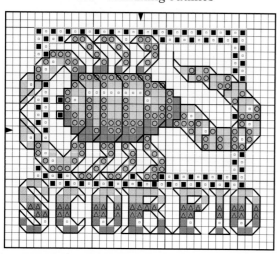

November 12

Design size: 30 wide x 30 high

	Anchor	DMC
	2	blanc
	386	3823
	361	738
	1002	977
	131	798
	351	400
	403	310

Backstitch:
268/469—stems
400/317—remaining outlines

November 13

Design size: 24 wide x 26 high

	Anchor	DMC
□	2	blanc
■	334	606
◉	314	741
■	328	3341
□	301	744
■	403	310

French Knot: 401/413
Backstitch: 401

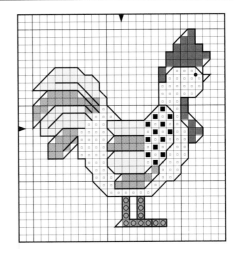

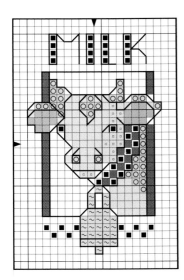

November 14

Design size: 18 wide x 29 high

	Anchor	DMC
■	24	963
~	311	3827
□	276	739
▫	367	738
◉	368	437
■	370	434
■	403	310

Backstitch:
370—cow (except eyes), bell
370 (2 strands)—border
403—lettering, eyes, collar

November 15

Design size: 33 wide x 33 high

	Anchor	DMC
□	2	blanc
■	46	666
■	1005	816
■	314	741
△	330	947
□	259	772
+	265	3347
■	268	469
■	96	3609
■	99	552
■	1002	977
~	1048	3776
■	1004	920
■	231	453
◉	232	452
■	233	451
■	403	310

Backstitch:
1005—apples (except stem)
268—pumpkin stem, leaves
101/550—grapes
403—teapot, pumpkin, apple & grape stems

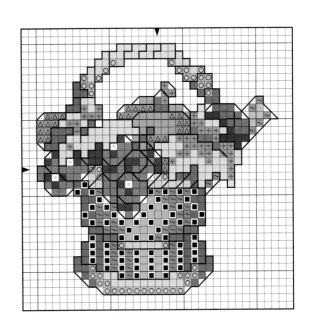

137

November 16

Design size: 27 wide x 30 high

	Anchor	DMC
▫	2	blanc
▨	24	963
≈	9	352
▨	11	351
☐	292	3078
▨	206	564
▨	2/231	blanc/453
◎	232	452
■	403	310

French Knots: 400/317
Straight Stitch (whiskers): 400
Backstitch:
210/562—leaves
400—remaining outlines

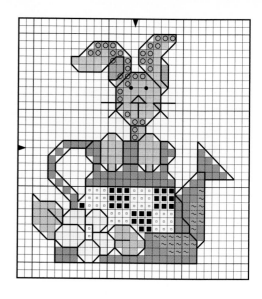

November 17

Design size: 44 wide x 23 high

	Anchor	DMC
▫	2	blanc
◎	885	739
▨	1012	754
△	9575	3830
▨	1013	3778
▨	240	966
▨	391	3033
≈	393	640
▨	234	762
■	403	310

Backstitch:
884/356—bulbs (except tops),
  pots, dirt
242/989—bulb tops
400/317—cat

November 18

Design size: 31 wide x 27 high

	Anchor	DMC
▫	2	blanc
▨	334	606
☐	1012	754
▨	891	676
≈	1002	977
◎	1003	922
■	403	310

French Knots: 403
Backstitch:
1024/3328—mouth
1013/3778—skin
400/317—diaper, chair, cat

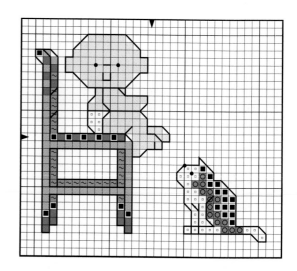

November 19

Design size: 30 wide x 30 high

Anchor	DMC
2	blanc
336	758
338	922
884	356
302	743
314	741
366	951
362	437
875	3813
876	3816
398	415
401	413

French Knots:
1024/3328—trees
400/317—door knob
Backstitch:
884—trees
877—frame, window
   panes
130/809—fence
400—remaining
   outlines

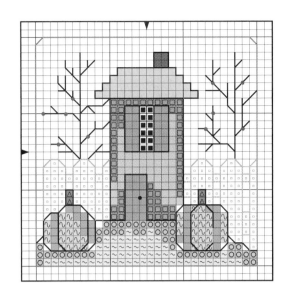

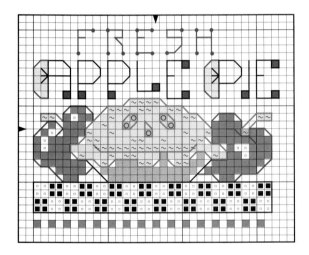

November 20

Design size: 33 wide x 26 high

Anchor	DMC
2	blanc
334	606
276	739
367	738
129	809
979	312
376	3774
403	310

French Knots: 1005/816
Backstitch:
1005—"FRESH," apple slice edges, apples
   (except stems)
979—"APPLE PIE"
379/840—pie crust, stems
400/317—dish
403—tablecloth

November 21

Design size: 30 wide x 27 high

Anchor	DMC
2	blanc
24	963
13	347
891	676
1012	754
1047	402
1048	3776
358	801
398	415
233	452
403	310

Backstitch:
13—her mouth
403—hats, belt, shoes, her collar, cuffs, & apron
358—remaining outlines

November 22

Design size: 25 wide x 30 high

	Anchor	DMC		Anchor	DMC
□	2	blanc		129	809
	1012	754		136	799
	868	353	△	881	945
~	313	742	✕	1047	402
♡	329	3340		1048	3776
	301	744		1084	840
	240	966			
◇	216	502			
	158	747			
◉	167	519			

French Knots: 400/317
Backstitch:
217/561—tendrils
400—remaining outlines

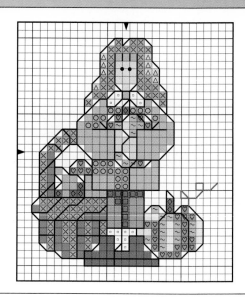

November 23

Design size: 13 wide x 44 high

	Anchor	DMC
	1023	3712
	6	754
⊡	386	3823
	214	368
	120	3747
~	1047	402
	1048	3776
	234	762
✕	399	318
■	403	310

French Knots: 403
Backstitch:
349/301—eggs, leaf
403—black bird
400/317—remaining outlines

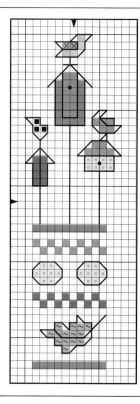

November 24

Design size: 30 wide x 30 high

	Anchor	DMC		Anchor	DMC
□	2	blanc	♡	129	809
	1012	754		136	799
	868	353		370	434
▢	311	3827	■	403	310
~	300	745			
	293	727			
◉	1043	369			
△	206	564			
	208	563			
✕	160	827			

Backstitch:
130/809—wind
403—eyes, buttons
400/317—remaining
　outlines

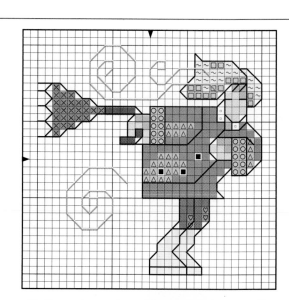

November 25

Design size: 41 wide x 23 high

	Anchor	DMC
▫	2	blanc
■	334	606
▨	253	472
□	128	800
▨	130	809
□	885	739
▨	361	738
◎	362	729
△	368	437
▨	234	762
■	403	310

French Knot: 403
Backstitch:
365/435—dog
(except nose)
370/783—brown
bones
403—nose
400/317—remaining
outlines

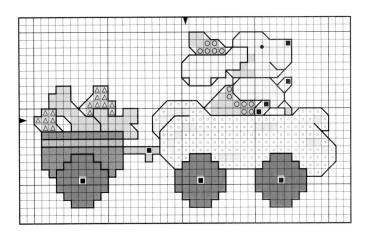

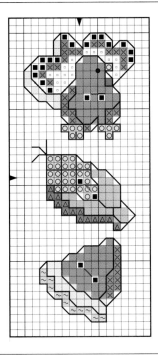

November 26

Design size: 15 wide x 38 high

	Anchor	DMC
▫	2	blanc
■	334	606
◎	305	743
▨	240	966
◩	226	703
□	128	800
□	933	543
~	368	437
▨	1002	977
☒	1048	3776
■	403	310

French Knot: 403
Backstitch:
334 (2 strands)—thread on corn button
211/562—corn husk
211 (2 strands)—thread on turkey & pie buttons
371/434—turkey, corn kernels, pie

November 27

Design size: 19 wide x 39 high

	Anchor	DMC
□	48	3689
▫	74	3354
◎	300	745
▨	206	564
□	342	211
□	366	951
~	368	437
▨	235	414

French Knots: 235
Backstitch:
210/562—leaves
235—remaining outlines

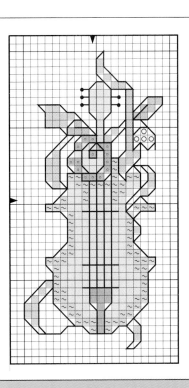

November 28

Design size: 24 wide x 41 high

	Anchor	DMC
	2	blanc
	48	3689
	50	605
~	1012	754
+	868	353
	259	772
△	265	3347
	267	469
	311	3827
○	1047	402
	1049	3826
	381	938

Backstitch:
50—flower
1013/3778—skin
265—wings
267—ribbons, leaves
1049—hair, gem, dress, "TOPAZ"
403/310—eyes

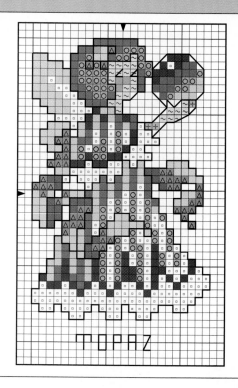

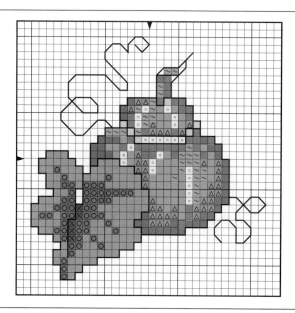

November 29

Design size: 32 wide x 32 high

	Anchor	DMC
	314	741
△	330	947
	333/1004	608/920
	300	745
	302	743
~	265	3347
	267	469
	875	3813
○	877	3815
✕	1044	895

Backstitch:
341/918—pumpkin (except stem), tendrils
267—stem
1044—leaf

November 30

Design size: 21 wide x 32 high

	Anchor	DMC
	2	blanc
	334	606
	361	738
~	363	436
	1072	992
	370	434
	900	648
■	403	310

French Knot: 403
Backstitch:
370—lettering, straw
400/317—remaining outlines

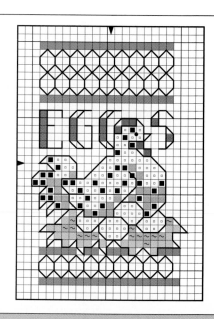

December

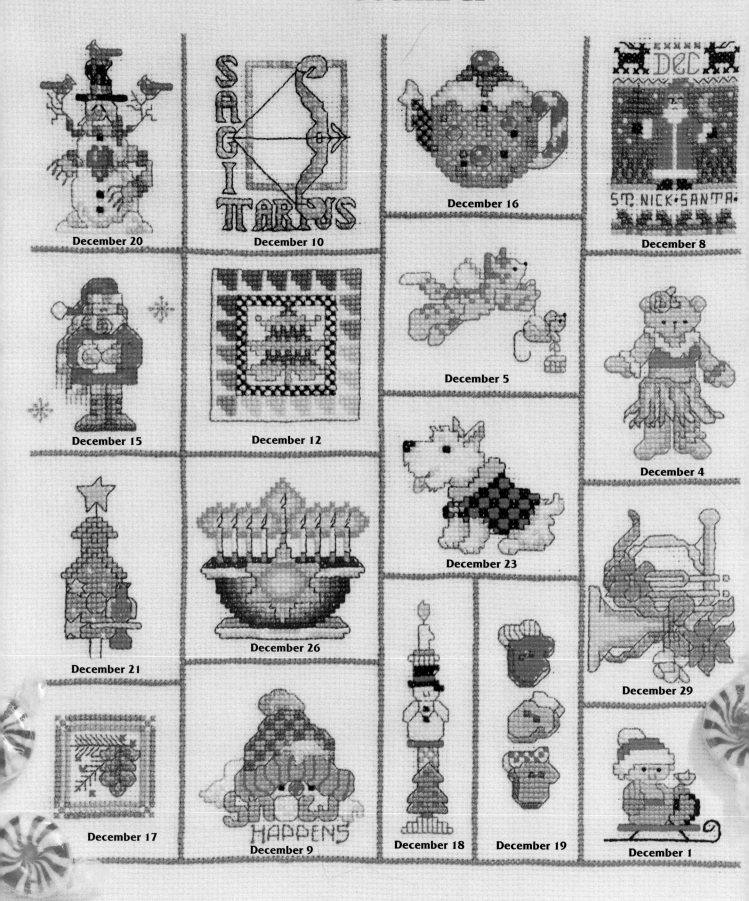

December 20

December 10

December 16

December 8

December 15

December 12

December 5

December 4

December 21

December 26

December 23

December 29

December 17

December 9

December 18

December 19

December 1

December

December 2

December 28

December 11

December 25

December 3

December 22

December 24

December 14

December 13

December 7

December 30

December 31

December 27

December 6

December 1

Design size: 23 wide x 22 high

	Anchor	DMC
▫	2	blanc
■	334	606
□	1012	754
□	302	743
▨	225	702
□	128	800
▨	96	3609
▨	399	318
■	403	310

French Knots: 403
❙ **Backstitch (2 strands):** 403
Backstitch:
1024/3328—mouth
1013/3778—skin (except nose)
146/798—bird
349/301—shirt stripes, nose
403—boots
400/317—remaining outlines

December 2

Design size: 29 wide x 30 high

	Anchor	DMC
▨	328	3341
▨	333	608
≈	9046	321
■	1005	816
□	259	772
▨	265	3347
△	257	905
■	246	986

French Knots: 9046
Backstitch:
9046—"Poinsettia"
1005—flower,
   "DECEMBER"
44/815—border
257—flower center
246—leaves, stem

December 3

Design size: 22 wide x 21 high

	Anchor	DMC
▫	2	blanc
□	24	963
■	334	606
□	361	738
□	1001	976
⊚	370	434
□	234	762
■	235	414
■	403	310

Backstitch:
371/434—dog (except ears, eye, & nose)
400/317—hat, ears
403—eye, nose

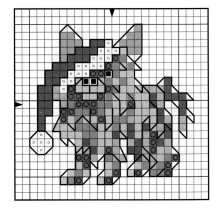

December 4

Design size: 26 wide x 34 high

	Anchor	DMC
▨	333	608
⊠	302	743
□	1043	369
△	241	966
□	103	211
⊚	96	3609
□	881	945
≈	1047	402

French Knots: 403/310
Backstitch:
210/562—leaves, skirt
1049/3826—bear (except nose)
400/317—remaining outlines

December 5

Design size: 33 wide x 24 high

Anchor	DMC	French Knots: 403/310
2	blanc	**Backstitch:**
1012	754	33/3706—cheese bow
338	922	884/356—cat (except
300	745	wings), cheese
311	3827	130/809—wings
128	800	400/317—remaining
234	762	mouse

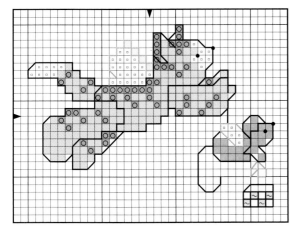

December 7

Design size: 13 wide x 18 high

Anchor	DMC	French Knots: 403
2	blanc	**Backstitch:**
334	606	334—hat stripes
323	3825	334 (2 strands)—thread
361	738	370/434—nose, broom
254	3348	handle
209	913	400/317—remaining
128	800	outlines
369	435	
403	310	

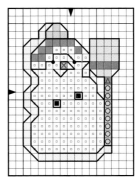

December 6

Design size: 28 wide x 30 high

Anchor	DMC	Anchor	DMC
2	blanc	361	738
27	899	1047	402
46	666	1048	3776
1005	816	**French Knots:** 936/632
316	970	**Backstitch:**
300	745	1005—bow, berries,
302	743	ornaments, red candy
241	966	211—leaves
209	913	110—purple candies
211	562	936—bells, hangers,
108	210	cookies
110	208	

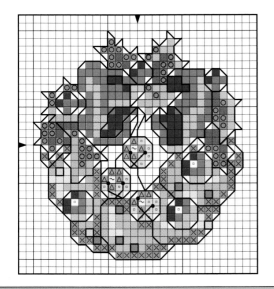

December 8

Design size: 25 wide x 38 high

Anchor	DMC	French Knots:
2	blanc	147/797—"ST."
13	347	403—word separations
868	353	**Backstitch:**
891	676	13—"DEC," mouth
205	912	218—tree
218	319	147—zigzag lines,
146	798	remaining lettering
403	310	403—antlers, eyes, nose

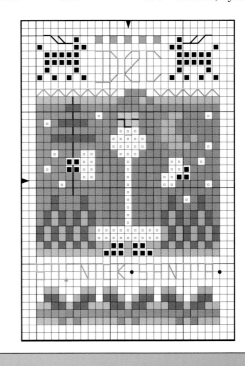

December 9

Design size: 33 wide x 30 high

	Anchor	DMC
◦	2	blanc
■	334	606
▨	323	3825
▨	1092	995
△	186	959
□	128	800
~	129	809
◉	146	798
■	403	310

French Knots: 146
Backstitch:
334 (2 strands)—hat stripes
130/809—snow
146—"SNOW HAPPENS"
400/317—remaining outlines

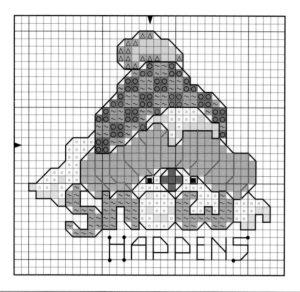

December 10

Design size: 28 wide x 34 high

	Anchor	DMC		Anchor	DMC
□	311	3827		342	211
◉	1002	977		109	209
▨	1049	3826			
~	260	772			
▨	261	989			
▨	876	3816			

Backstitch:
109—border
403/310—remaining outlines

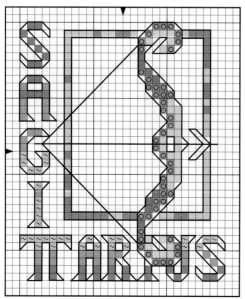

December 11

Design size: 21 wide x 29 high

	Anchor	DMC
◦	2	blanc
■	334	606
▨	225	702
▨	129	809
▨	234	762

French Knots: 403/310
Backstitch:
334—ark cabin stripes, candy cane stripes
245/986—tree
400/317—remaining outlines

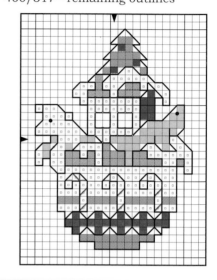

December 12

Design size: 30 wide x 30 high

	Anchor	DMC		Anchor	DMC
◦	2	blanc	▨	130	809
□	313	742	△	131	798
▨	260	722	⊠	347	402
▨	262	3363	■	403	310
□	128	800			

Backstitch: 400/317

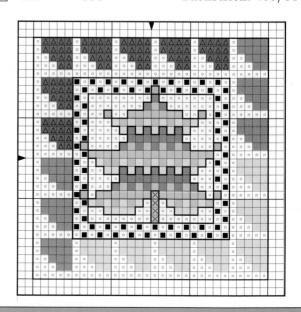

December 13

Design size: 30 wide x 23 high

Anchor	DMC
893	224
895	223
300	745
891	676
206	564
208	563
366	951
347	402
400	317

French Knots: 334/606
Backstitch:
211/562—leaves
400—remaining outlines

December 14

Design size: 35 wide x 31 high

Anchor	DMC
2	blanc
73	963
75	962
334	606
361	738
363	436
1043	369
241	966
210	562
129	809
349	301
234	762
403	310

French Knots: 403
Backstitch:
76/961—tongue
211/562—tree
371/434—dog (except face), snowman nose & arms
400/317—remaining snowman, dog mouth, scarf, earmuffs
403—dog eyes & nose

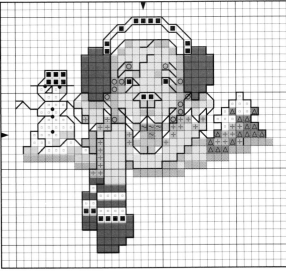

December 15

Design size: 28 wide x 30 high

Anchor	DMC
2	blanc
333	608
9046	321
1012	754
1043	369
241	966
130	809
378	841
399	318
400	317

French Knots:
130—snowflakes
400—eyes
Backstitch:
130—snowflakes, scarf fringe
400—remaining outlines

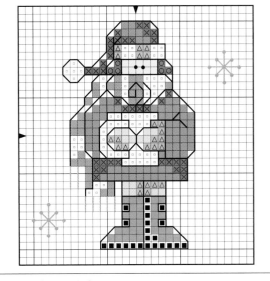

December 16

Design size: 34 wide x 27 high

Anchor	DMC	Anchor	DMC
2	blanc	108	210
27	899	110	208
46	666	403	310
1005	816		
311	3827		
1003	922		
1048	3776		
238	703		
228	700		
246	986		
128	800		

Backstitch:
1005—red berries, handle
246—leaves, green dots
131/798—frosting
111/553—purple dots
1004/920—teapot
403—black dots

December 17

Design size: 20 wide x 20 high

Anchor	DMC		Anchor	DMC
□ 2	blanc		⊙ 347	402
■ 334	606		■ 379	840
~ 361	738		**Backstitch:**	
■ 875	3813		**210/562**—branch	
✕ 876	3816		936/632—cone	
■ 977	3755			

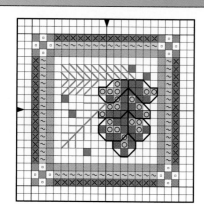

December 18

Design size: 10 wide x 46 high

Anchor	DMC
□ 2	blanc
■ 334	606
□ 305	743
■ 225	702
■ 130	809
■ 403	310

Backstitch:
334—base stripes
245/986—tree
146/798—candleholder stripes
349/301—flame
400/317—remaining outlines

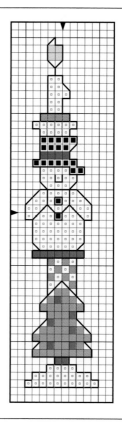

December 19

Design size: 13 wide x 37 high

Anchor	DMC
□ 2	blanc
■ 334	606
■ 1005	816
□ 254	3348
△ 256	704
□ 128	800
~ 129	809
✕ 146	798
■ 400	317

Backstitch:
334 (2 strands)—threads on green
& blue mittens
257/905—red mitten cuff stripes
257 (2 strands)—thread on
red mitten
400—remaining outlines

December 20

Design size: 26 wide x 38 high

Anchor	DMC
2	blanc
9	352
1025	347
44	815
324	721
891	676
227	701
9159	828
1039	518
162	517
358	801
234	762
235	414
400	317
403	310

Backstitch:
44—heart
227 (2 strands)—scarf fringe
358—scarf, branches, birds, nose
235—snowman (except face)
403—hat, mouth, buttons
403 (2 strands)—eyes

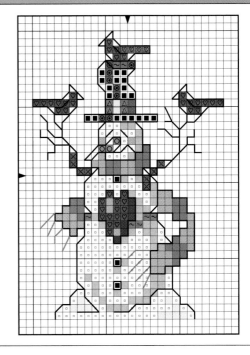

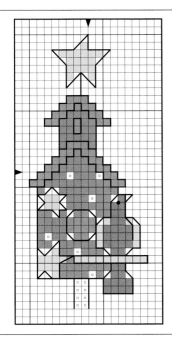

December 21

Design size: 16 wide x 36 high

Anchor	DMC
2	blanc
333	608
305	743
130	809
399	318

French Knot: 401/413
Backstitch: 401

December 22

Design size: 27 wide x 32 high

Anchor	DMC
334	606
4146	950
914	407
1042	504
875	3813

Eyelets (stars): **136/799**
Backstitch:
211/562—needles
400/317—remaining outlines

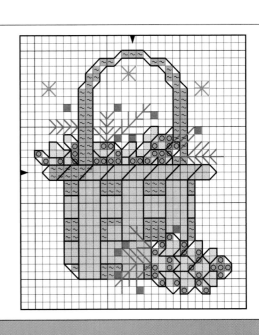

December 23

Design size: 32 wide x 27 high

	Anchor	DMC
▫	2	blanc
▨	74	3354
▨	334	606
▫	302	743
▨	234	762
◉	399	318
■	403	310

Backstitch:
76/961—tongue
400/317—dog (except eye & nose)
403—eye, nose, coat

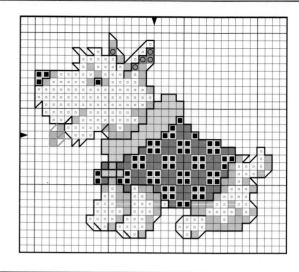

December 24

Design size: 23 wide x 40 high

	Anchor	DMC
▫	2	blanc
⊠	47	321
▨	328	3341
▨	334	606
▫	300	745
▨	891	676
▨	240	966
△	215	320
~	9159	828
▨	1038/1039	519/518
▫	128	800
■	403	310

Backstitch:
136/799—snow
403—bird's eye
400/317—remaining outlines

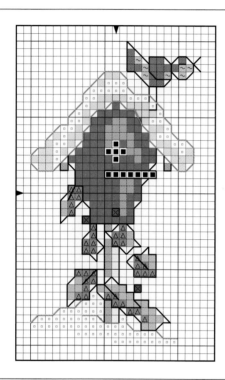

December 25

Design size: 37 wide x 34 high

	Anchor	DMC
▫	2	blanc
■	46	666
▫	311	3827
▨	240	966
△	242	989
~	928	3811
▨	129	809

French Knots:
146/798—snowflake
400/317—snowman

Backstitch:
46—scarf fringe, box (except letter)
146—hat cuff, snowflake
400—remaining outlines

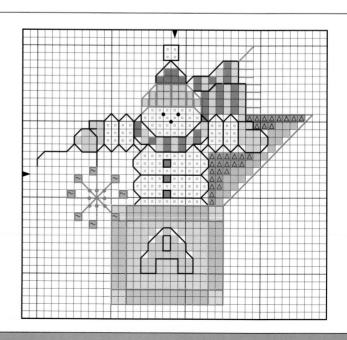

December 26

Design size: 35 wide x 32 high

Anchor	DMC
2	blanc
301	744
313	742
324	721
9159	828
130	809
131	798
133	820

Backstitch:
131—top left edges of flames
133—remaining outlines

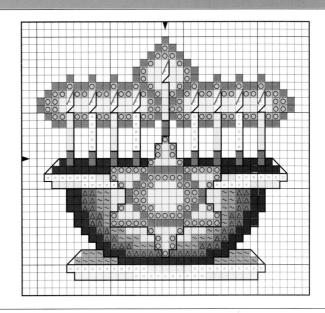

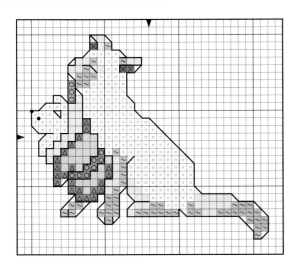

December 27

Design size: 32 wide x 27 high

Anchor	DMC
2	blanc
1092	995
186	959
95	554
96	3609
1012/9575	754/3830
337	3776
884	356

French Knots: 403/310
Backstitch:
884—big cat (except eye & nose)
400/317—kitten, mitten
403—big cat eye & nose

December 28

Design size: 23 wide x 43 high

Anchor	DMC
2	blanc
50	605
46	666
1006	304
1012	754
868	353
1092	995
185	964
187	958
189	943
259	772
265	3347
262	3363
336	758
338	922

Backstitch:
1006—berries
1013/3778—skin
187—gem, dress
189—"TURQUOISE"
265—wings
269/936—holly leaves
340/920—hair
403/310—eyes

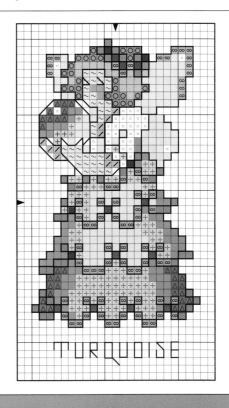

December 29

Design size: 29 wide x 34 high

	Anchor	DMC
▫	2	blanc
▣	1023	3712
▢	301	744
⊠	362	437
⊙	214	368
▣	875	3813
△	876	3816
▢	128	800

Backstitch: 400/317

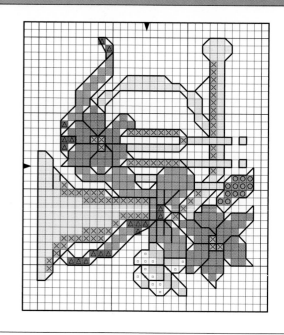

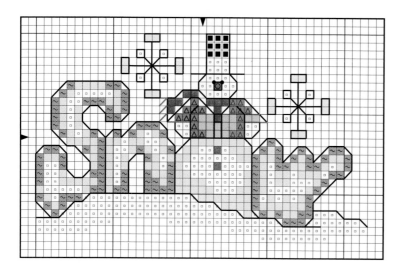

December 30

Design size: 43 wide x 26 high

	Anchor	DMC
▫	2	blanc
⊙	40	956
▨	1098	3801
▢	1042	504
△	215	320
▢	128	800
~	129	809
■	400	317

French Knots: 400

Backstitch:

1098—scarf fringe, sleeve stripes

136/799—snowman (except nose),
    lettering, snow, flakes

400—remaining outlines

December 31

Design size: 48 wide x 26 high

	Anchor	DMC
▫	2	blanc
▢	24	963
◣	334	606
▢	305	743
▢	204	563
▨	96	3609
▢	361	738
~	349	301
△	1003	922
■	403	310

French Knots: 403

Backstitch:

38/961—cat nose

349—bell, cat (except paws, face,
    & whiskers)

400/317—mouse, paws, collar

403—eyes, whiskers, mouth

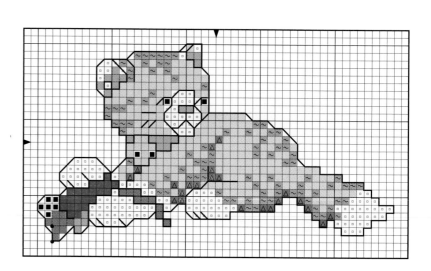

General Directions

THE MATERIALS

The materials required for counted cross stitch are few and inexpensive: a piece of evenweave fabric, a tapestry needle, some six-strand cotton floss, scissors, and a charted design. An embroidery hoop is optional. All of these products are readily available at needlework departments or shops.

FABRIC

For counted cross stitch embroidery we use "evenweave" fabrics which are woven with the same number of horizontal and vertical threads per inch. Cross stitches are made over the intersections of the horizontal and vertical threads, and because the number of threads in each direction is equal, each stitch will be the same size and perfectly square. A fabric is described by the number of threads per inch; that number is called its thread count.

The thread count and the number of stitches will determine the finished size of a stitched design. Fabric with a higher thread count will produce a small design (more stitches are worked per inch) and a lower thread count will produce a larger design because there are fewer stitches per inch.

Evenweave fabrics commonly used for cross stitch are Aida cloth, linen, an array of specialty fabrics, and waste canvas. There are also many kinds of pre-made evenweave products.

Aida Cloth is a cotton fabric that has groups of four threads woven in a basketweave pattern, making the intersections very easy to see. Aida is woven in several sizes, measured by the number of squares: 11-count (11 stitches per inch), 14-count, 16-count, and 18-count. The most commonly used Aida is 14-count.

Linen is woven of single threads. Cross stitches are made over two threads in each direction. Linen is available in a variety of thread counts. Because the stitches are worked over two threads, the number of stitches per inch will be half the thread count. For example, on 28-count linen, you will work 14 stitches to the inch, the same finished size as if the design was worked on 14-count Aida.

Specialty Fabrics are woven in the same manner as linen, but may be cotton, synthetic, or a combination of fibers. These fabrics will have different thread counts and may be known by different names, depending on the manufacturer. There are also some non-fabric surfaces that are popular for counted cross stitch. Vinyl-Weave™ is a vinyl product that looks like Aida cloth, is waterproof, and does not ravel. Perforated paper is a pressed paper with small round holes and stitches are made over the spaces between the holes; it is somewhat fragile. Perforated plastic is a plastic canvas that looks like perforated paper but is structurally stronger.

Waste Canvas can be used if you wish to cross stitch on a non-evenweave surface, such as clothing. It is a temporary evenweave product that is available in a variety of thread counts. Baste a piece of waste canvas onto the surface to be cross stitched, work over the canvas threads, then remove the canvas threads after the stitching is complete.

Pre-made Products are very convenient if you want to stitch a towel, pillow, or baby bib, but you don't like to sew. Most pre-made products incorporate evenweave fabric (usually Aida) as part of their construction. These products have a pre-determined amount of space available for stitching. When working on pre-mades, be sure the design you select will fit on the product before you begin stitching.

Use the chart below as a guide to determine the approximate finished width and height of a stitched design based on the count of your chosen background fabric.

	Number of Stitches in Design				
Thread Count	10	20	30	40	50
11-count	1"	1¾"	2¾"	3⅝"	4½"
14-count	¾"	1⅜"	2⅛"	2⅞"	3⅝"
16-count	⅝"	1¼"	1⅞"	2½"	3⅛"
18-count	½"	1⅛"	1⅝"	2¼"	2¾"

(measurements are given to the nearest ⅛")

THREADS AND NEEDLES

The most commonly used thread for counted cross stitch is six-strand cotton embroidery floss. It can be divided to work with one, two, or more strands at a time. Separate the floss into individual strands, then put the required number back together before threading the needle.

Most of these designs were cross stitched on 16-count Aida cloth with two strands of floss. The 16-count fabric allows the true color intensity to show. A few designs were stitched on 14-count fabric, vinyl, or perforated plastic. On 14-count fabrics, two strands of floss are usually used, but the color will be less intense because the background fabric is slightly visible. On 14-count perforated surfaces, three strands are recommended because the space over which the stitch is made is relatively small. On 18-count fabrics, one strand of floss is used.

A small blunt-tipped tapestry needle, size 24 or 26, is used for stitching. The higher the needle number, the smaller the needle. The correct size needle is fairly easy to thread with the amount of floss required, but not so large that it will distort the fabric. The chart below tells you which size needle is appropriate for each size of Aida cloth and suggests the number of floss strands to use.

Fabric	Stitches Per Inch	Strands of Floss	Tapestry Needle Size
Aida	11	3	22 or 24
Aida	14	2	24 or 26
Aida	16	2	24, 26 or 28
Aida	18	1 or 2	26 or 28

Our photographed models were stitched with Anchor six-strand embroidery floss, and DMC floss numbers are also listed. The companies have different color ranges, so these are only suggested substitutions. If a color is used for a specialty stitch but not a cross stitch, the color numbers are listed (Anchor is first) separated by a slash mark.

A "blended" color produces close color shading for cross stitching. A blend is noted in the color key as two numbers separated by a slash mark; use one strand of each color.

WORKING FROM CHARTED DESIGNS

Counted cross stitch designs are worked from charts, with each square representing the space for one cross stitch. The design stitch width and height are given; centers are shown by arrows. The color in each square shows the floss color to be used for the stitch. The chart colors are not necessarily close matches for the floss colors. They have been charted to provide contrast for ease in reading the charts. Often a symbol is added to the color square to provide even more contrast. The chart is accompanied by a color key which lists the numbers of the floss colors to be used.

Decorative stitches are also shown on the charts. Straight lines over or between squares indicate backstitches or straight stitches. Eyelets are shown by their shape, and French knots by dots. Occasionally color is used for lines and dots to help differentiate the colors to be used. For other charts, a thicker line is used for further clarification.

GETTING STARTED

Cut floss into comfortable working lengths; we suggest about 18". To begin in an unstitched area, bring threaded needle to front of fabric. Hold an inch of the end against the back, then anchor it with your first few stitches. To end threads and begin new ones next to existing stitches, weave through the backs of several stitches. Trim thread ends close to fabric. Wherever possible, end your thread under stitches of the same color and toward the center of the design.

THE STITCHES

Note: Use two strands of floss for all cross stitches and one strand for backstitches, straight stitches, French knots, and eyelets, unless otherwise noted in the color key.

Cross Stitch

The cross stitch is formed in two motions. Follow the numbering in **Fig 1** and bring needle up at 1, down at 2, up at 3, down at 4 to complete the stitch. Work horizontal rows of stitches, **Fig 2**, wherever possible. Bring thread up at 1, work half of each stitch across the row, then complete the stitches on your return.

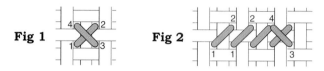

Fig 1   Fig 2

When a vertical row of stitches is appropriate for the design, complete each stitch then proceed to the next as shown in **Fig 3**. No matter how you work the stitches, make sure that all crosses slant in the same direction.

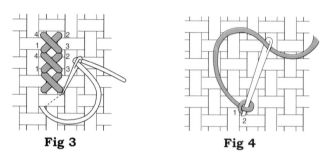

Fig 3   **Fig 4**

French Knot

Bring thread up where indicated on chart. Wrap floss once around needle, **Fig 4**, and reinsert needle at 2, close to 1, but at least one fabric thread away from it. Hold wrapping thread tightly and pull needle through, releasing thread just as knot is formed. For a larger knot, use more strands of floss, but wrap only once.

Occasionally, the color key will use colored dots to help differentiate the floss colors to be used.

Backstitch

Backstitches are worked after cross stitches have been completed. They may slope in any direction and are occasionally worked over more than one square of fabric. **Fig 5** shows the progression of several stitches; bring thread up at odd numbers and down at even numbers.

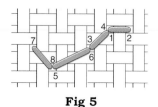

Fig 5

Frequently you must choose where to end one backstitch color and begin the next color. As a rule of thumb, choose the object that should appear closest to you. Backstitch around that shape with the appropriate color, then backstitch the areas behind it with adjacent color(s). Occasionally, a color key will have two backstitch symbols (a thick line and a thin one), or colored lines to help you differentiate colors.

Straight Stitch

A straight stitch, **Fig 6**, is made like a long backstitch. Come up at one end of the stitch and down at the other. The length and direction of these stitches will vary—follow the chart for exact placement. Be sure to secure thread well at the beginning and ending of a group of straight stitches so they stay taut.

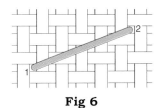

Fig 6

Eyelet

This is a technique that produces a starburst effect. Bring thread up at any point along the outside of the charted shape, **Fig 7**, and stitch down into the center. Continue to work around the shape as shown on the chart, always entering at center of eyelet.

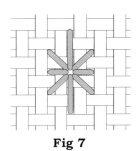

Fig 7

Occasionally, the color key will use colored lines to help differentiate the floss colors to be used.

PLANNING YOUR PROJECT

You can work any of the designs alone as a small project, two or three as companion pieces, or you can combine similar designs to cover a larger surface. However you choose to use the designs, the planning process will be the same.

Select your chart and type of fabric. Determine the finished dimensions of the stitched area. Divide the number of stitches in width by the number of stitches per inch of fabric. This tells you how many inches wide the design will be. Repeat for the height of the design. Or, for an approximate size, refer to the table on page 155. If you are working an arrangement of several designs, we recommend you draw the outlines, or mark outside dimensions, on a piece of graph paper before beginning to stitch.

Add enough additional fabric for desired unworked area around the design plus an additional 2" or 3" on each side for use in finishing and mounting. If you are using a pre-made item, make sure there is a large enough stitching area available.

Cut your fabric exactly true, even with the weave. Some ravelling may occur as you handle the fabric while stitching. To minimize ravelling, along the raw edges use an overcast basting stitch, machine zigzag stitch, or masking tape (to be cut away when you are finished).

Ideally, the progression of your work should be from left to right and from the top of the design toward the bottom. With this sequence, you will bring your thread up from the back to the front through unoccupied fabric holes and will stitch down from front to back through already occupied holes, thereby disturbing completed stitches as little as possible.

FINISHING NEEDLEWORK

Most needleworkers love to stitch, but tend to get bogged down with the finishing process. It need not be so. While most projects are framed, there are many easy (and inexpensive) ways to finish your work, especially with these delightful tiny designs.

When you have finished stitching, dampen your embroidery. If soiled, wash stitched fabric in cool water with a gentle soap. Rinse well. Roll in a towel and squeeze out excess moisture. Place face down on a dry towel or padded surface and iron carefully. Make sure all thread ends are well anchored and clipped closely.

We have shown a variety of easy finishing products on our photographed models, including Sudberry House's Shaker pincushion, Darice perforated plastic, Ramco Arts' acrylic accessories, gold frames from Yarn Tree, Framecraft's porcelein box, wire hangers from Country Wire, and snowglobe, Addition, towel, and jar lid from Crafter's Pride. Simple assembly (if any) is required for these items.

To make perforated plastic ornaments, stitch the design, then cut excess plastic at least one space beyond all stitches. Glue a larger piece of felt to the wrong side with a hanging loop in between, then trim felt edges with pinking shears. Follow the same procedure for the plant poke, except omit the hanging loop, then glue the end of a wooden dowel to the back of the felt.

Sources

Shaker Pincushion:
Sudberry House
12 Colton Rd
East Lyme, CT   06333
1-800-243-2607

Perforated Plastic (14-count)**:**
Needlecraft Shoppe
23 Old Pecan Rd
Big Sandy TX   75755
1-800-259-4000

Acrylic Coasters:
Ramco Arts
Fort Worth, TX   76180
1-817-281-3733

Small Gold-tone Frames:
Yarn Tree
1-800-247-3952

Porcelain Box:
Framecraft
Ann Brinkley Designs
3895B Oracle Rd.
Tucson, AZ   85705
1-800-633-1048

Wire Hangers:
Country Wire
Michell Marketing
3525 Broad St.
Chamblee, GA   30341
1-770-458-6500

Snowglobe, Addition, Towel, Jar Lid:
Crafter's Pride
Daniel Enterprises
PO Box 1105
306 McKay St.
Laurinburg, NC   28353
1-800-277-6850

Design Index

This index will help you locate designs by subject matter.
Numbers refer to the design's page number.

(continued on page 160)